9
THE LAST LIBERAL

Dave Carley

THE LAST LIBERAL

The Last Liberal
first published 2006 by
Scirocco Drama
An imprint of J. Gordon Shillingford Publishing Inc.
© 2006 Dave Carley

Scirocco Drama Editor: Glenda MacFarlane
Cover design by Terry Gallagher/Doowah Design Inc.
Author photo by Michael Lee
Printed and bound in Canada

We acknowledge the financial support of the Manitoba Arts Council, The Canada
Council for the Arts and the Government of Canada through the Book Publishing
Industry Development Program (BPIDP) for our publishing program.

Production inquiries should be addressed to:
Pam Winter
Gary Goddard Agency
10 St. Mary Street, Suite 305
Toronto, Ontario M4Y 1P9
(416) 928-0299
goddard@canadafilm.com

Library and Archives Canada Cataloguing in Publication

PS
8755
, A748
L38
2006

Carley, Dave, 1955-
    The last liberal/Dave Carley.

A play.
ISBN 1-897289-05-7

    I. Title.

PS8555.A7397L38 2006   C812'.54   C2006-902867-2

J. Gordon Shillingford Publishing
P.O. Box 86, RPO Corydon Avenue, Winnipeg, MB Canada R3M 3S3

For Joan and Bob McRae

Dave Carley

Dave Carley is a Toronto-based playwright, screenwriter and editor. His plays have had over three hundred productions across Canada, the USA, and a dozen other countries around the world. They include Scirocco Drama's *The Edible Woman*, *Orchidelirium*, *Midnight Madness* and *Writing With Our Feet*. Real to Reel Productions has just completed production on *Yours, Al* (written with Bill Spahic) for broadcast on CBC TV's Opening Night program. *The Final Hour*, written with Glenda MacFarlane, was a finalist this past year for a Canadian Screenwriting Award. Dave is currently working with the Shaw Festival on a new drama about Danish playwright Kaj Munk. Dave's website is www.davecarley.com.

Acknowledgements

The playwright wishes to thank the GCTC cast and crew for their help in developing this script, as well as the following individuals and institutions: Great Canadian Theatre Company, Alan Borovoy and *The New Anti-Liberals*, Simon Bradshaw, Margaret Carley, Mary Lou Chlipala, Betty Jane Giles, Annie Kidder, Glenda MacFarlane, Charles McFarland, Paul Malette, Micheala Murphy, Lorne Pardy, Sheila Perry, Gordon Shillingford, and Martin Ship. Also the participants in a Toronto reading in February, 2005: Meg Hogarth, Aaron Hutchinson, Marcia Johnson, Darren Keay, Charles McFarland, Kristopher Turner, Michael Waller and Richard Waugh.

Production Information

The Last Liberal was commissioned by Ottawa's Great Canadian Theatre Company. It was first workshopped at that theatre in October, 2003, with Charles McFarland (Director) and actors Simon Bradshaw, Kevin Klassen, Maureen Smith, David Warburton and Beverley Wolfe.

A week-long workshop was held in September, 2004 with the following participants:

BARBARA Rankin	Terry Tweed
RON Bloom	Richard Waugh
SARA Munro Bloom	Maureen Smith
MARC Bloom	David Coomber
ZIMRAN Vettur	Hamza Adam
SAM Grearson	Michael Mancini

Director: Charles McFarland
Assistant to Director: Patrick Gauthier

The Last Liberal premiered at Ottawa's Great Canadian Theatre Company on April 28, 2005. In addition to the cast, director and assistant director from the September, 2004 workshop, participants included:

Set, Costume and Lighting Design: Stephen Degenstein
Sound Design: Jon Carter
Stage Manager: Shainna Laviolette
Assistant Stage Manager: Kevin Waghorn,
who also played "Chad" and the voice of Bill DeClute
Voice of Premier: Richard Mahoney
Sound Design: Jon Carter

Characters

RON Bloom—age 40
SARA Munro Bloom—age 40
MARC Bloom—age 15
BARBARA Rankin—age 50-something
ZIMRAN Vettur—age 17
SAM Grearson—age 30
(Sam can also play the offstage voices of
BILL DeClute and PREMIER.)

Time and Setting

The time of the play is over a period of a few months, in the very near future. The settings are varied.

Notes on Staging

The staging should be fluid, with no blackouts between scenes. I have numbered the scenes and described their locales for clarity in the rehearsal process, but not to suggest any kind of break in the action.

Zimran speaks perfect English; no accent is necessary. If anything, his speech is a bit formal. His clothing can be suggestive of a non-Western religious affiliation, but not specifically that of any group. In this draft, the Premier is referred to as male—but the offstage voice, which presumably is pre-recorded, could just as logically be that of a female with all the attendant pronoun changes in the script.

Rhythmically, the characters often cut over each other. Cutovers are indicated by a sentence with no period, with the next character's speech beginning with a dash (-).

Act One

Scene 1
The TV Studio's 'Breakfast with Sara' set. Now.

> *Stage is in darkness. There can be intro music; a peppy theme song—maybe from SARA's show. It dies down to just a tinny memory as a door opens and a woman is silhouetted in light. She begins scrabbling at the wall.*

BARBARA: Damn. Early again. Damn. Where the jumping hell is the light switch

BILL: *(Offstage; miked.)* -It's on the right.

> *BARBARA is taken by surprise.*

Ma'am. The right. It's on the right.

BARBARA: On the (right)— Story of my goddamn life.

> *BARBARA finds the light, turns on set lights. She looks about for BILL.*

Who—where the heck are you?

BILL: Sorry. Bill DeClute. Up here in the booth.

BARBARA: Oh right, hi. *(Waves.)*

BILL: Sara phoned. She's running a bit late. If you want coffee there's a machine down the hall but it uses city water and after the scare last week…

BARBARA: Ashburnham water, nooo thanks. I'll just make myself at home. *(Goes over to set.)* Bill? Before Sara gets here—I've got a question—Bill? Bill—you still there?

BILL:	Just a sec… Yeah—you were asking
BARBARA:	- I've got a question
BILL:	- Fire away

SARA bursts in.

SARA:	- Sorry sorry, I hate being late whoahhh
BARBARA:	What.
SARA:	The jacket.
BARBARA:	What about it?
SARA:	It's bright, that's all. It'll pull focus—off me. Can't have that! What've you got under it—sure, that's fine, that blouse is good. Sorry I wasn't here—thank you for coming—Barbara, get this: I got up at the crack of dawn, I actually made the guys breakfast. Bacon and eggs and now they're out golfing—Marc and Ron, golfing! How Norman Rockwell is that!? Six months ago if someone'd told me— It's like a dream come true. What a journey it's been—for all of us—
BARBARA:	Journey isn't quite the word I'd use.
SARA:	Maybe not but
BARBARA:	- About face, yes, U-turn, uh huh, one-eighty
SARA:	- Barbara. It's water under the bridge.
BARBARA:	You think?
SARA:	This morning at least. This show is about you. Bill, are you ready?
BILL:	Yes ma'am.
SARA:	You know that Ron and I have the deepest respect for you. We know how—disenchanted you still are. But let's keep it upbeat, upbeat gets the dollars and if we can put your fundraising drive over the top, that'd be terrific

BARBARA:	- I understand
BILL:	- Five minutes.

SARA is fitting BARBARA with a lapel mike.

SARA: We'll keep it simple. Biographical. Then you can make the pitch; we'll run a clip of the library—Bill went up there on the weekend and got some nice footage—I'll present the cheque from the station—Lord where's the cheque, I left it on my desk, damn *(Starting to get up to get it.)* We'll have a little presentation, then Barbara, Barbara, if you can possibly say something about Ron, something positive that is, slip in a few words, if you can, hold your nose, and then we'll get back to you, especially the Plevna angle.

BARBARA: You really want to talk about Plevna?

SARA: Absolutely. It's where the library is. You've still got family there, right?

BARBARA: The place is nothing but family. Rankins up the ying-yang

SARA: - Ron's very weak north of Highway 7. Up there, they'd vote for road kill if it was Tory. They'd vote for it, then they'd eat it. Just kidding. Anyway, we'll talk about the library, a bit about Ron, we'll praise Plevna unto the bloody hills, you can tell us about growing up north of the IQ line *(Has started to exit, turns back.)* That was a joke about the IQ line.

BARBARA: Ron says it all the time too.

SARA: Ron does not. He does?

BARBARA: It actually wears a little thin.

SARA: He'll stop. We can't go around offending half our riding, even if it's the half that doesn't vote for us.

SARA exits.

BARBARA: She seems a little hyper.

BILL: She's always like that before her show. So—you had
                 a question?

BARBARA: - Yes—I was wondering if you

                          SARA flies back in.

SARA: Oh listen, we got off on the wrong foot again—we
                 always do. Right from the day Ron became Minister
                 we've been sniffing each other like two old
                 bitches—it's my fault, I never dreamt I'd have to
                 hand my husband over to another woman,
                 especially such a capable one and… Barbara. I'm an
                 uptight pain in the ass. That's why Ron's in politics
                 and not me. And this is about Ron. It's going to be
                 tight. Last election was a squeaker for us and,
                 depending on whom the Tories and NDP nominate
                 next week, this one could be even tighter. So forget
                 about me, concentrate on Ron.

BARBARA: I thought this was about the school library.

SARA: Well of course it is. And that's why I'm going to get
                 that cheque.

                          SARA exits.

BARBARA: Bill?

BILL: Yes.

BARBARA: Do you freelance?

BILL: It's my middle name.

BARBARA: I need to tape a public service announcement—I
                 was wondering if you could do it, if I find a room
                 somewhere

BILL: - We can use this studio

BARBARA: Really?

BILL: It's part of my contract with Sara—I can use the
                 studio anytime.

BARBARA: Good. Because, as the lady said: It's been quite the trip, these past few months since Ron got re-elected. A real goddamn journey…

Scene 2
Six months earlier—Ron's Victory Celebration.

> *Back in time. Balloons and banners. RON is at the mike, with SARA at his side. BARBARA might be watching from the sidelines.*

RON: Well, that was a bit close for comfort. I haven't been so nervous since the day I married Sara.

> *SARA swats him good-naturedly.*

Thank you all for your hard work—I'll start naming names in a minute but first and foremost—my family. Sara—my wonderful, supportive wife who, contrary to the Tories' claims, never once used her television station to unfairly promote my candidacy. *(Sotto, to laughter:)* Not.

> *SARA waves, to cheers.*

Sara's the brains behind this operation. The only reason she's not your MPP is I'm the one who needs gainful employment. I'd also like to thank my son, Marc—he's somewhere out there—Marc—well he's around—and also my mother, Pearl, champion envelope-stuffer. Friends, I know you want to start the party so I'll be quick. It is truly an honour to go back to Queens Park for a second term to represent the riding of Ashburnham—both the city—and the county—

> *A few jeers at "county".*

Now come on. We did get some votes outside the city.

SARA: Twelve.

RON: But who's counting. And I'm sorry that we don't seem to have won a majority at Queens Park this time out—it looks like we've fallen a few seats short, but rest assured we will continue to bring this province back to sanity. Much of our last term was about repairing the damage caused by the Tories' so-called Common Sense Revolution. Now, with this new mandate, we can begin our own Liberal revolution. We can begin to show people what we're made of: compassion, a commitment to real equality and to use the power of the government to bring hope to the province's poor, to restore confidence in our health care system, and to bring back excellence to my area of concern, the public education system. This is so exciting, it is such a privilege to be part of this, I thank you from the bottom of my heart—

> *Cheers have been rising below the foregoing and crest. Stage fades to black. Perhaps last portion of RON's speech echoes.*

Scene 3
Ron's office, Queen's Park. A few weeks later.

> *Sudden light shift. RON turns to BARBARA. He is holding a champagne bottle.*

RON: Look what I found in the outer office! Perfect timing—we can toast my first week in Cabinet.

BARBARA: Why.

RON: I survived?

BARBARA: Barely.

RON: Aw come on

BARBARA: - Question period Wednesday? That's hardly surviving.

RON: You're bringing me down, man.

BARBARA: It was my fault.

RON: I'd love to blame you, Barbara, but in all honesty

BARBARA: - If you get nailed, it's my fault. That's what Executive Assistants are paid the big bucks for—we take the fall when our Ministers screw up.

RON: - I've only been here a bloody week. Nobody's blaming me.

BARBARA: Nooo. First they ask you if you favour standardized testing, which of course we do, duh, and then they spring the trap! Wham! You're squealing like a stuck pig! A whole ministry of educators and they go and buy a US test for the Grade Threes.

RON: It was my predecessor.

BARBARA: You're twisting in the wind. But it's good for us to start at the bottom. Though maybe we shouldn't sink too low, considering how wobbly this government is. There could be an election tomorrow.

RON: *(Struggling with bottle.)* You know how to work these?

BARBARA: Not if there's a cork. I'll get the glasses. In the meantime, you keep twisting. The cork.

RON: Thanks, by the way.

BARBARA: *(Full stop.)* For what.

RON: Everything.

BARBARA: That's OK. It's my job.

RON: You do it well. So thanks.

BARBARA: I should be thanking you.

RON: OK, this is getting out of control. But listen—bad first week or no, this is a nice gesture.

BARBARA: I didn't buy it. There isn't a bird on the label. Way
              out of my league. I assumed you bought it.

RON: *(Reading card.)* "Congratulations on your new
              portfolio. Sam Grearson."

BARBARA: Who the hell's that?

RON: Someone in the Ministry?

BARBARA: No. A constituent?

RON: Not that I know of.

BARBARA: Then he's a lobbyist. This building's infested with
              them. You wouldn't believe the stuff they sent the
              old Minister. They're usually more subtle.
              Champagne? What's next—strippers? I'll find out
              who it's from and send it back. But mark my words,
              Ron—another week and the outer office'll be lined
              with payola. Cuz "you de man" Ron. "You de man".
              Does your son say that?

RON: I don't think so, Dude Woman.

BARBARA: Well he should. Because you really are de man.

RON: Get lost.

Scene 4
Ashburnham High—The Principal's office.

              *ZIMRAN is very nervous. He holds a letter and
              mostly reads from it.*

ZIMRAN: Sir, I cannot attend that class. My spiritual welfare is
              not enhanced by dancing in a gymnasium full of
              jiggly girls wearing shorts and very little else. And
              the music is disgraceful. I do not know if you have
              listened to the words, sir, well, I am sure you have
              not because if you had, you would not allow such
              lyrics in your school. I can participate in the other
              phys-ed classes—for example, soccer—so long as I

am not required to wear shorts. I must wear track pants and a long-sleeved shirt. Sir, I am representing all the Malach students at Ashburnham High. We beg permission to be excused.

Scene 5
Ron's office again.

>   *BARBARA is bringing in some files and policy papers, or letters to be signed.*

BARBARA: Rumour has it you're a Cabinet Minister who reads...

RON: You said something earlier—we have very strict guidelines about gifts—are you saying my predecessor was accepting stuff?

BARBARA: My lips are sealed. I never comment on previous Ministers.

RON: Fair enough

BARBARA: - Had to watch him like a hawk. I've worked for five Ministers over the years, and that one nearly gave me a stroke, every day.

RON: Wow.

BARBARA: Four years ago I could've passed for twenty-five. Now I'm the goddamn Wreck of the Hesperus.

RON: I've been wondering—well, forgive me, but—well—for a job like this, aren't you—I mean, why

BARBARA: - Aren't I too old? I'm way too old! Yeah, I was all set to take the package and slink home to Plevna but—but then the election happened, I worked on your campaign, then you got Education, and I decided I wasn't so old after all and, anyway, we're from the same neck of the woods.

RON: Different sides of the IQ line.

BARBARA: OK, I don't want to hear that one again.

RON: Right right.

BARBARA: You need us. This government could fall next week and if you don't get us country folk on side, at least some of us, you're up the fecal creek. You had pretty weak opponents last time.

RON: No kidding. I only got in because all the NDP could find to run against me was a transsexual mime artist. Wal-Mart Greeter.

BARBARA: The fact you're in Cabinet now should help.

RON: Maybe.

BARBARA: *(Leaving, stops.)* Anyway. I'd read some of the stuff you wrote about the value of public education— that speech you gave to the Teachers Federation, that was amazing—so I decided to stay a bit longer. Just till you're Premier.

RON: Hang on!

BARBARA: - The Premier's not going to stick around. He hasn't got the temperament to govern with a minority. Then it's 'Hello Ron Bloom.'

RON: Oh no it's not. No no no no no

BARBARA: - Methinks my Minister doth protest too much.

RON: You thinks wrong. Education is enough. So, did you find out who that Sam Grearson is?

BARBARA: No—but I expect you will tonight, at the Premier's reception. It's gonna be wall-to-wall lobbyists. When does your wife arrive?

RON: As soon as she can get away from the station. She's driving down with Marc—hey, have you ever seen her show?

BARBARA: Of course. I get my mother to tape it.

RON: She mostly does it because of CRTC rules, you know, local content, but it's actually quite popular.

BARBARA: 'Breakfast with Sara' is very, very big in Plevna. We talk of little else. Because, Sara is de wife of de man. Even if we don't vote for him.

RON points 'Go' and BARBARA does.

Scene 6
Behind the High School gymnasium.

ZIMRAN is peeking through a gym window at the jiggly girls, his back to the audience. Aerobics-style music, muffled, comes from off. ZIMRAN might even be copying an aerobics move. MARC saunters in and sees ZIMRAN.

MARC: What're you looking at?

ZIMRAN: Nothing, I was just

MARC: *(Looking.)*—You like that eh.

ZIMRAN: No. A little.

MARC: Smoke?

ZIMRAN: I do not smoke, thank you.

MARC: Gum.

ZIMRAN: *(Hesitates; he's not allowed.)* Yes. Please. *(Takes one.)*

MARC: For a minute I thought you were going to say you didn't chew gum either.

ZIMRAN is contemplating the gum; unwraps and chews it.

You skipping?

ZIMRAN: Pardon?

MARC: You skipping phys-ed too?

ZIMRAN: I am excused.

MARC: How'd you swing that?

ZIMRAN: It is against my religion.

MARC: *(Laughs.)* Mine too. Thou shalt not fucking exercise. *(Beat; realizes his mistake.)* Whoah. You're serious.

ZIMRAN: I can exercise but not if it is dancing. Badminton is acceptable. Soccer is very good. *(Beat.)* But I must not dance with girls to improve my health.

MARC: Aerobics sucks anyway. Cool hat.

ZIMRAN: *(Has never thought of it that way.)* Really? Thank you. It is a harq.

MARC: How come yours is white and the guys in the stores have blue ones?

ZIMRAN: I am not a man yet.

MARC: When do you become a man?

ZIMRAN: When I marry.

MARC: When's that?

ZIMRAN: Next year. When I'm 18.

MARC: Whoah. *(Pulls out a doob, or rolls it during following.)*

ZIMRAN: Why are you not in aerobics?

MARC: The music's fucked.

ZIMRAN: That is a good enough reason?

MARC: It is for me.

ZIMRAN: But do you not need a permit to leave? *(Produces his.)*

MARC: I just don't go. They don't care. Sometimes I skip the whole day. No one checks. You're supposed to hand that to the teacher, you know.

ZIMRAN: I offered it to him but he said, "It is OK, we will keep you away from these naughty jiggly girls." Everybody laughed.

MARC: He's an asshole.

> *MARC lights his doob. ZIMRAN is fascinated; he wants to smell it and doesn't move away. At some point MARC will offer it to him—not really believing he'll take it—and ZIMRAN refuses, of course. But he's sure breathing the air.*

I've seen you before, sitting here. Every time I see you, you are alone. Why is that, if I may ask?

MARC: I only talk to people when it suits me. And it doesn't suit me very often. OK, Mr. Questions: every time I see you, you're with a crowd of Malachs. What's with that?

ZIMRAN: We are to be accompanied at all times.

MARC: Like you're policing each other?

ZIMRAN: *(Beat. An admission. He has, in fact, thought of it this way.)* Yes.

MARC: That's fucked. Listen. I'm going downtown—want to come?

ZIMRAN: Now?

MARC: Why not. I've got to meet someone. Let's go before your 'posse' arrives.

ZIMRAN: But my permit only lets me out of phys-ed.

MARC: So?

ZIMRAN: The naughty girls are almost done jiggling and then unfortunately I must go to Biology. Who are you meeting downtown?

MARC: A customer. So I'll see you around. *(Exiting.)*

ZIMRAN: What is your name?

MARC: Marc. Bloom.

ZIMRAN: Mine is Zimran. Vettur. Hey Marc. Thank you for
               talking to me.

               *MARC swaggers off. ZIMRAN watches him leave,
               then turns around and walks in the other direction,
               maybe trying a bit of the swagger himself or maybe
               not quite yet.*

Scene 7
Before the Premier's reception:
Sam's house, the park and Ron's office.

               *Light up on SAM, having fun with hair gel. He is
               facing a mirror and has managed to spike his hair in
               a trendy look. Suddenly he attacks his head,
               flattening the do back down.*

SAM: What are you thinking!

               *Light fades on SAM as he conservativizes his hair,
               and comes up on SARA.*

SARA: (Pacing, outside in a park. She is looking around, sees no
               one, and dials her cell phone.) Come on. Come on.
               Where are you? Ronnnn.

               *Light comes up on BARBARA. She picks up the
               phone in RON's office.*

BARBARA: Minister Bloom's line.

SARA: Can you tell him I'm running late.

BARBARA: Hi Sara.

SARA: Hi. Hi Barbara.

BARBARA: How late?

SARA: I'm still in Ashburnham.

BARBARA: (Checks watch.) Oh-Kay.

Light fades off SARA as she hangs up. Light on RON, who is practice-putting.

That was your wife.

RON: She's running late?

BARBARA: Very late. She hasn't left for Toronto yet.

RON: She say why?

BARBARA: No.

RON: Must be Marc.

Light fades off them and back up on SAM, who has now progressed to his tie.

SAM: Help. Helllp. Help? I NEED HELP. I'm such a spazz. Please, can you help me with my tie? If you help me with my tie I'll fix the tap first thing tomorrow, I promise. Can you just come in and help me just for a second and—(*Takes a drink.*) Never mind.

Lights fade on poor SAM and up on SARA again. She is still in the park, pacing and looking. She dials RON. Light up on him and BARBARA. She stares at the call display.

BARBARA: It's your wife again.

RON: (*Picks it up.*) Hi honey.

RON moves off a bit from BARBARA.

SARA: He's nowhere to be found. He wasn't at school, he's not at home, I've checked the mall, I'm at the park right now

RON: - You haven't left Ashburnham?

SARA: No.

RON: Which means

SARA: - I'm not going to get there in time.

RON:　　　　Honey

SARA:　　　- I'm sorry but I can't—find—Marc. And I'm not leaving here until I do.

RON:　　　　This is kind of key, this thing tonight. It would be nice to be the perfect nuclear family—you and me with Marc. You can bet the Premier's daughter will be there.

SARA:　　　Falling off her chair.

RON:　　　　I need you, at least. Let him roam, whatever, we can deal with him tomorrow.

SARA:　　　No.

RON:　　　　You can leave him a note and

SARA:　　　- I'm not leaving him alone.

RON:　　　　*(Beat.)* Why would you be checking the park?

SARA:　　　*(Beat.)* He hangs out here.

RON:　　　　Which park—the one downtown?

SARA:　　　Yes.

RON:　　　　Why the hell's he—? Are you sure he's not at school? Maybe there's a football game and he's gone to watch

SARA:　　　- Marc watching football? "That's so fucked".

RON:　　　　It was a longshot.

SARA:　　　Can't you take Barbara? She'd love to go.

RON:　　　　She's already going.

SARA:　　　Go together. By the way, I was kind of rude to her earlier, can you apologize for me? *(Beat.)* Ron, we have to talk about Marc.

RON:　　　　I know.

SARA:　　　This weekend, when you're home. I love you. Bye.

Light off SARA. BARBARA has heard some of the last.

RON: She's not coming—Marc's gone AWOL again and she doesn't want to leave town. I don't know what's wrong with that kid. It's one thing after another.

BARBARA: Boys are like that.

RON: Not all boys.

BARBARA: My brothers were hellions.

RON: When I was Marc's age, I went to school, I came home, I did my homework, Thursday and Friday nights I helped out at Dad's store, weekends I was golfing. And even the golfing was to please Dad. Your brothers were really wild?

BARBARA: Legendary.

RON: And they turned out OK?

BARBARA: Eventually. Jail helped.

RON: Do you want to be my date for the Premier's thing?

BARBARA: I thought you'd never ask. I'm going to dash home and change into something less comfortable. Meet you there?

Light off them and up on SAM. He is putting a different shirt and tie on.

SAM: I forgot to tell you, the bank phoned. We got the loan. You can call in the roofers. Let's sink further into debt, yea! (*Notices there's no response.*) Oh oh. (*Goes to door.*) No no no, we really do need a new roof. I want a new roof. (*He doesn't.*) Hey—I still need help with my tie. Steeeve. Please? (*Goes to the door.*) This is the tie that makes the lobbyist look good who gets the nod who makes the bucks who pays for the roof who—are you giving me the finger? (*Laughing.*) You're going to pay for that. (*Heading off.*) When I get home, you're going to pay.

Scene 8
Outside the Premier's reception.

> *RON is waiting for BARBARA. Better dressed than before. Smiling etc. at people going in. BARBARA hurries up, a bit dishevelled. BARBARA is no fashionista.*

BARBARA: Sorry. It took me ages to find the jacket—it was under my jeezly bed. Your tie's crooked, let me get that. *(Straightens it.)* So listen. Everyone's going to be watching you. Your reactions.

RON: Because he's resigning, I know. Don't worry—I won't stand up and cheer.

BARBARA: *(Under.)* No that's not it

RON: - And I'll try not to look consumed with ambition because

BARBARA: - He's not quitting.

RON: Of course he's quitting. He's an autocrat—he doesn't want to have to cut deals with the NDP just to stay Premier. And this is totally his style—his inaugural reception, he makes the grand announcement, leaves before he's pushed, looking like a visionary who's got the best interests of the party at heart. After you went home, I got a call from the Star, they'd heard from the same place I'd heard and

BARBARA: - I hope you acted sad!

RON: I am sad.

BARBARA: In the future refer the media to me.

RON: My wife owns a bloody TV station, I think I know how to handle them.

BARBARA: Ron, with all due respect, you haven't seen a microphone yet you didn't want to stick up your ying-yang.

RON: Ms Rankin, your images.

BARBARA: You say too much to them.

RON: I'm just being honest.

BARBARA: Exactly. Refer them to me. Now. I talked with my source in the Premier's office. My source says he's not resigning tonight, no way. Apparently the Premier just wants to find the right issue and then go back to the polls A.S.A.P. He's convinced the voters are in a cold sweat because they didn't elect a Liberal majority. So tonight—for starters—he's announcing that he's protecting the entire greenbelt north of Toronto—right down to the last bloody tree—that's two seats back to us next election. And he's planning to build a couple of hospitals up north, including a French one. Un hôpital. Two more seats. He's nearly there.

                SAM has appeared and sees them. They don't notice him.

RON: What are you saying—all my hopes and dreams are dashed?

BARBARA: I wish you'd be serious.

RON: I don't want to be Premier.

BARBARA: Of course you do.

RON: I don't.

BARBARA: You do.

RON: You sound like my wife. How do you guys know what I want when it hasn't even crossed my mind?

BARBARA: You should be Premier. What's he got that you don't have?

RON: I am a better golfer.

BARBARA: So then get this: my source in the Premier's office tells me the minute he wins a majority—he's quitting! Goes out a champion. It's all about his penis.

RON: You've been a very busy Executive Assistant.

BARBARA: It's why I'm paid the big bucks. Now, let's go in.

RON: OK. What's the word we're supposed to say when we enter a room? That makes us look happy and confident? Cheese?

BARBARA: Majority.

RON: *(With her.)* Majority.

> *Smiling, they enter the reception. SAM follows.*

Scene 9
The Bloom's basement.

> *It's a pretty typical basement-type family room, and is MARC's home. SARA enters.*

SARA: Marc? Marc? You down here? Marc! *(Sees that he's not home yet. Dials cell phone.)* Ron—hi, it's me, when you get home, call me. It's uh ten-fifteen. He's not home yet. I'll be up. *(Hangs up, then dials again.)* Me again. Hope it went well tonight. Did you remember to act sad? Love you.

> *SARA leaves kiss, hangs up again and sits down. She sees MARC's knapsack—and is clearly tempted to look in it.*

Marc? Marc?

> *No answer again. SARA opens the knapsack and almost immediately finds MARC's stash. It's a big stash.*

Oh God. Oh God. *(Under her breath.)* Jesus look how much, oh God, oh God. *(Finds Ecstasy pills.)* Oh no, oh no.

> *SARA replaces the stuff in the knapsack. Keeps it close to her. There's a noise; MARC is coming through the window.*

What the—

> *MARC is fully in and sees SARA.*

MARC: Jesus, you scared me.

SARA: I scared you?! How long have you been coming in that way?

> *MARC shrugs. He registers his knapsack being very close to SARA.*

Did you forget that tonight was the Premier's reception?

MARC: I hate that shit.

SARA: You agreed to go.

MARC: You and Dad agreed I'd go.

SARA: I was looking all over town for you.

MARC: You should've gone without me.

SARA: *(Pulls out his stash.)* What, and leave you with this?

MARC: You've been going through my stuff!

SARA: Did you think I wouldn't find out?

MARC: It's not like you're ever around. *(Starts to leave.)*

SARA: *(Grabs him.)* Get back here.

MARC: Let go.

SARA: Marc, talk to me. There's a lot of stuff here. This is way more than for just you. Are you pushing?

MARC: Is that the problem?

SARA: It's a different problem, it's a worse problem, yes it's a problem if you're pushing

MARC: OK it's all for me. Personal use. Does that make you
               happy?

SARA: No. And I don't believe you. And I phoned your
               school today, they said you were in class and I asked
               them to go look and you weren't there, then they
               found a note from your father, your father who
               hasn't been here in a week, so now you're forging
               notes on his letterhead, you've been seen at the
               park, so I went downtown, you weren't there—
               where were you, who are you selling to, are you
               selling to the kids at school—where are you going,
               Marc, Marc, get back here!

               MARC pushes by her, and quite forcefully pulls his
               knapsack out of her grip, pushing her back in the
               process.

               MARC! MARC!

               Fast black.

Scene 10
After the Premier's reception.

               A political after-party. BARBARA and RON are
               standing together amid the buzz. She has a beer.

BARBARA: Tell me that wasn't a campaign speech.

RON: It was definitely upbeat.

BARBARA: Like Up With People on uppers.

               SAM is approaching.

               I need a refill. You want anything?

RON: Naw, I'm trying to project a sober, unambitious
               image.

               BARBARA leaves and SAM swoops in.

SAM: Minister?

RON doesn't turn.

Minister Bloom?

RON: Oh sorry—you mean me. I'm a Minister now aren't
           I.

SAM: *(Shaking hands with him.)* I'm Sam Grearson.
           Congratulations on your appointment.

RON: Thank you.

SAM: You don't mess around—one term on the
           backbench, then the biggest portfolio…

RON: It helps when half the caucus got wiped out in the
           election. Sorry, I didn't get your name.

SAM: Sam Grearson.

RON: Aha. It was you who sent

           *BARBARA has noticed SAM and has made a U-
           turn.*

           - Hey—I've found him. Champagne Sam. She's
           going to tell you that we really can't accept that sort
           of thing. The new payola guidelines are very strict.
           But I appreciate the gesture. My Dad used to give
           bottles of Manischevitz to his best customers every
           Christmas. It was very ecumenical—a teetotalling
           Jew giving out crates of the undrinkable to thirsty
           Gentiles. In their hour of greatest need.

BARBARA: Who are you with?

SAM: Sorry, I'm Sam Grearson.

           *SAM outstretches his hand. BARBARA doesn't take
           it.*

BARBARA: Who are you with?

SAM: Uh—the Foundation for Independent Education.

RON: Private schools.

SAM: That's not our term, sir. "Private" suggests exclusion and we're all about opportunity. But that's a whole other discussion, isn't it, and not one we should get into here

BARBARA: - Not one we should get into anywhere.

Awkward silence.

SAM: What did you think of the Premier's speech, Minister?

RON: Please, Ron. Uh—it was very inspiring. We're all pumped. Aren't we Barbara. Pumped? Barbara tells me all the right words to say.

BARBARA: Like 'shoo.'

Another awkward pause.

SAM: There'd been talk he was stepping down.

RON: Ah no, not a chance. He's a fighter. He's going to lead us back into the fray. Any day now.

SAM: *(Laughs.)* Hopefully not too soon.

RON: You never know with minority governments.

SAM: Well, I just wanted to congratulate you on your appointment and surviving your first week

RON: What—you call that thing on Wednesday surviving?

SAM: It won't hurt kids to know that Washington was the first president.

RON: Unfortunately, the question was, 'Who was our first president'.

SAM: Forgotten by Monday. Nice to meet you, Ms—I didn't get your name

BARBARA: You know who I am.

RON: Barbara Rankinrude.

SAM: Of course. The celebrated Barbara Rankin. I hear congratulations are in order—not many Executive Assistants get libraries named after them.

RON: What's that?

BARBARA: I'll tell you later.

SAM: OK then. *(Turns to leave; then, elaborately casual.)* Say, Minister—I hear you're a bit of a golfer.

RON: I am, a bit.

SAM: You interested in eighteen some time? Glen Abbey?

RON: No kidding. Sure.

SAM: Great. I'll call your office next week, set something up. Nice to meet you both.

> *SAM moves off.*

RON: What. What're you staring at?

BARBARA: I'm looking for his pointy tail.

RON: What's this about a library?

BARBARA: Never mind.

RON: Tell me.

BARBARA: Back home. A project I took on after the Tory cuts. We're building a school library

RON: - Right, I heard about that—I didn't know they were naming it after you.

BARBARA: If you'd actually go to Plevna sometime…

RON: If anyone from there would actually vote for me sometime.

BARBARA: They only just decided to name it after me. How the hell he knew that

RON: - He's a smart cookie.

BARBARA: He's a snake.

RON: Yeah, but a snake who golfs at Glen Abbey.

>   *Lights off them.*

Scene 11
The park downtown, later at night.

>   *MARC is sitting on the bench. ZIMRAN is walking through the park.*

MARC: Hey. Vettur. Zimran! It's Marc.

ZIMRAN: Hello.

MARC: You're alone. I thought that was illegal.

ZIMRAN: I was closing up the store. My father said I could walk home.

MARC: You need permission to walk home? That is really fucked.

ZIMRAN: Last year my cousin was beaten up here.

MARC: Yeah, it was in the papers, that was sick. I went to the rally. My Dad spoke at it.

ZIMRAN: Why are you here?

MARC: Had a fight with my mom. You in a hurry?

ZIMRAN: *(Hesitates, then sits.)* I often fight with my father.

MARC: I would with mine if he was ever around. What do you guys fight about?

ZIMRAN: I tell him I cannot do my homework if I have to work at the store every night.

MARC: That is so fucked up.

ZIMRAN: He does not even like me going to school.

MARC: You're actually fighting with your father because you want to do homework. Are you insane?

ZIMRAN: Very insane. It is from the lack of aerobics.

MARC laughs.

My father is very strict. He is the senior Malach here, he knows all the laws, he has to set an example.

MARC: Sounds like you're the example.

ZIMRAN: *(Beat; again, he's thought of this.)* Yes.

MARC: Do you ever want to just say "fuck it"?

ZIMRAN: *(Pause.)* Yes.

MARC: Me too.

ZIMRAN: Sometimes I would like to watch television.

MARC: You can't watch TV?

ZIMRAN: Of course not. It's against our religion.

MARC: We sponsored a Malach family. When they first came to Canada. My parents, our whole family actually, it was like a project. I guess that's not the right word, yeah, they were our fucking "project". They lived in our basement.

ZIMRAN: That was very kind of you.

MARC: My Mom did all the work. Their name was Vettur too.

ZIMRAN: All our last names are Vettur.

MARC: They only stayed for a couple of months, then they got their own place. That was two years ago. You guys are Muslims, right?

ZIMRAN: No. Muhammad is important to us, but no more so than Jesus. And the way we eat—the best way to describe it is kosher. We're a mix; it's because of where we lived, we took on all the religions, Malachs were traders and

MARC: - So what would you watch, if you had one. Homework shows?

ZIMRAN: Comedies. They are the best way to learn contemporary English.

MARC: If you want to talk like a fucking American.

ZIMRAN: Exactly. And I would like a cell phone. And my own computer, not just the one at the store that everyone uses. And my own iPod.

MARC: Take mine. (*As ZIMRAN begins to refuse.*) Just a loaner. I've got another at home. Why not.

> *ZIMRAN takes it quickly and puts it in his pack.*

ZIMRAN: Thank you Marc. I should go. In case father comes along. He wouldn't be happy if he caught me

MARC: - You're just sitting here.

ZIMRAN: He would not see it that way. (*Starts to leave.*) Are you going to stay here all night?

MARC: Naw, I'll go home eventually.

ZIMRAN: I did not see you at school all week.

MARC: I skipped most of it. But listen, I'm here a lot of nights. Stop by.

> *They do some kind of handshake thing, which ZIMRAN gets wrong.*

This way.

> *ZIMRAN gets it right.*

Yeah. You're a fast learner.

> *ZIMRAN exits, maybe swaggering a bit, happy.*

Scene 12
Ron's office, a week later.

> *RON is putting while BARBARA hectors him and/ or sends back the balls to him.*

BARBARA: You can't go tomorrow.

RON: It's Glen Abbey!

BARBARA: I don't care if it's Pebble jeezly Beach, you shouldn't go golfing with him.

RON: Nothing bad has ever happened on a golf course.

BARBARA: I thought that private school thing was settled last year. When we cut off their tax credits, I thought that was it—no more favours to that bunch, but now they're back. Slicker than ever.

RON: Our Sam is not slick. He's actually a bit pathetic. He called three times this week to confirm.

BARBARA: He's getting you on the golf course where you're vulnerable. I bet he even lets you win, just to pump up your ego, and then when you hit the 19th hole he'll ply you with liquor

RON: - Barbara. Three things: Policy is policy, we're not funding private schools, we're not giving them tax breaks, they don't need them, we can't afford to give them. Two: I'm not going to be plied with drinks after the game—I might have a beer but then it's back to Ashburnham to open that new Seniors Home. And most important: no one "lets me win." Haven't you read my CV? Junior Champ, Ashburnham Golf and Country, married to the Girls' Junior Champ—golf is the central narrative of my life. Golf—and women ordering me around.

BARBARA: I've researched Grearson's Foundation and it's the unholiest alliance since Hitler and Stalin. They've got Islamic Fundamentalists, Orthodox Jews,

Christian Creationists, French Immersionists and they've topped it all off with rich WASP bastards.

RON: All of whom are taxpayers! At the very least they deserve the pretense of being listened to. And if I can do that on Canada's best course…

BARBARA: *(Beat.)* It's none of my business but shouldn't you be going home instead of playing golf?

RON: It is none of your business.

BARBARA: Sara's phoned about Marc every day this week.

RON: That's private. That's there. You look after things here. Let me golf in peace and raise my family as I see fit.

Black.

Scene 13
The Vetturs' electronics store.

MARC saunters up to the counter where ZIMRAN is working.

MARC: Hey.

ZIMRAN: Hi.

MARC: Thought I'd check out your store. I didn't realize you sold all this stuff. I mean, considering you can't watch TV or listen—and what's with the razors? When did your Dad last shave?

ZIMRAN: *(Really nervous.)* How are you?

MARC: Fine. How are you?

ZIMRAN: I'm fine also but

MARC: - Because I'm excellent

ZIMRAN: - My father is in the basement and he will be up in a minute and

| MARC: | - I get you. Stop by the park later. |

They do the handshake thing; ZIMRAN has it right this time. Fast black.

**Scene 14
Woody's Bar.**

SAM is sitting with a drink. Bar noise in background.

SAM: *(Dials cell phone.)* I'm at Woody's, just for one, then I'll be home, I promise. Can you do me a favour—can you throw my golf shirt in the wash, maybe iron it a little bit, thank you thank you. Sorry, a call's coming in. *(Takes incoming call.)* Hello? Hello?

Light up on BARBARA.

BARBARA: It's Barbara Rankin. I'm phoning to confirm your golf game with the Minister tomorrow.

SAM: Yes, we've arranged to meet there. Why are you really phoning?

BARBARA: Don't get fancy.

SAM: Fancy?

BARBARA: Stick to golf.

The noise spikes a bit; maybe some laughter.

Where are you?

SAM: I'm having a drink.

BARBARA: The Minister doesn't drink, by the way. It sounds like you're in a bar.

SAM: I am. Is that a problem?

BARBARA: I thought Christian-Muslim-Jews didn't go to bars.

SAM: I'm none of the above. I'm a lobbyist who enjoys a drink.

BARBARA: Well don't take Ron there.

SAM: Uh, not to worry. It's not that kind of bar.

BARBARA: What—it's a gay bar?

SAM: Yup. Woody's. I won't bring him here, Ms Rankin, I promise. Lot of voters here though.

BARBARA: It's not his constituency.

> *BARBARA hangs up.*

SAM: Why don't I just shut my mouth. OK, one more. Chad!

Scene 15
The park.

> *Later that night. ZIMRAN and MARC are sitting on the bench. Both have knapsacks.*

MARC: Why were you so nervous today?

ZIMRAN: My father doesn't like us talking to people, unless they're customers.

MARC: So next time I'll pretend to be buying a razor.

ZIMRAN: He's the senior Malach and I'm the oldest son so

MARC: - I know. You're on display.

ZIMRAN: Like a top of the line personal care electronic item. The ones we keep in the locked case.

MARC: Me too. No, actually I'm a top of the line marketing tool. Like a billboard. 'Perfect son of perfect family- Vote for Ron Bloom.'

> *MARC pulls out joint. Which makes ZIMRAN very nervous. Offers it to ZIMRAN.*

ZIMRAN: No thank you. *(Of the iPod.)* This is enough Malach crime for now.

MARC: You never smoke.

ZIMRAN: No. But I like getting offered.

               Flashing lights off.

MARC: *(Freezing. Not so tough all of a sudden.)* Shit. *(Gets rid of doob. Slips it into his knapsack or flicks it away.)*

ZIMRAN: What.

MARC: Cops. By the statue. I've got a shitload of shit in there.

ZIMRAN: What do you mean?

MARC: Stuff. Shit. Jesus

ZIMRAN: OK my friend, I am going now.

               Takes MARC's knapsack.

MARC: What're you doing!

ZIMRAN: Malachs never do anything bad, remember.

               ZIMRAN gives MARC the handshake and walks off. MARC pulls ZIMRAN's bag closer. Also grinds out the joint. And then looks up.

MARC: Hello officer. Lovely evening. Lovely weather to be sitting in the park. Clean out my pockets? Sure…

               And MARC at this point realizes he has a pocket full of Ecstasy. Black on him as he mouths "Oh fuck."

Scene 16
Sam's house.

               SAM is getting dressed for the golf game. He holds up golf shirt.

SAM: Oh man. Steve. Steve?

               (Goes to door.) Steve, I love you I really do but I can't

wear this with the Minister of Education. A shirt
with a little bunny on the front and *(Turns shirt.)*: "I
can't even swing straight"? That's OK for the Pink
Putters League, but this is Glen Abbey. Thanks for
ironing it. I just can't wear it. *(Then.)* Can I wear your
sports shirt, the one with the little hippo? No
answer. He's mad. Great. *(Then.)* God I hate my life.

Scene 17
The Police Station.

> *MARC is sitting on a bench. Slam of doors etc. and
> SARA bursts in.*

SARA: Are you OK, oh Marc

MARC: *(Pulls back.)* -I'm fine.

SARA: They didn't hurt you or anything?

MARC: I'm fine.

> *Pause. They eye each other.*

             Can we go?

SARA: Pardon?

MARC: Can we go?!

> *Pause.*

SARA: Do you realize where you are? You're in a goddamn
             lockup, what, you think I can just walk in and spring
             you, you think that's how it works? Are you crazy?

> *No answer.*

> *(Closer to him; quieter.)* Are you OK? Are you high?
> Do you need a doctor or anything, you can get
> medical

MARC: - I just want to get the fuck out of here.

SARA: You can drop that tone, right now. I can't get you
            out. Not yet. I haven't called your father—I'm not
            sure what I'm going to tell him. Let's start with you
            telling me what happened. They're charging you
            with possession for the purpose of trafficking, so
            what did you have on you?

MARC: Some E, some pills, maybe a dozen hits. I forgot I
            had it in my coat.

SARA: There was nothing else—no marijuana? Where's
            your knapsack? The cops said they saw someone
            else leaving; they think you switched knapsacks,
            who were you with

MARC: - This place is bugged.

SARA: No it's not.

MARC: Duhh.

SARA: You're pissing me off.

MARC: Yeah, well I'm in the fucking jail, you come in and
            start giving me shit right, you don't even ask if I'm
            guilty or not, you just assume it, you just assume I'm
            shit. I want to get out of here, Mom, get me out of
            here.

SARA: They have to charge you first.

MARC: When.

SARA: I don't know. I never had a son arrested for
            trafficking before. I don't know the procedure.
            Probably tomorrow.

MARC: But you'll get me out tonight, right?

                   Pause.

SARA: No. No, I won't.

MARC: Call Dad. He will. Do you know how bad this looks
            on him?

SARA: Yes, I know exactly how bad it looks and what's
               more, I know how bad it is. And I'm not calling your
               father. He'll be home tomorrow. Tomorrow
               afternoon actually. He can deal with it then. Until
               then, you can just—sit there—you just sit there and
               do some thinking, you do some serious thinking.
               (Gets up and starts exiting.)

MARC: *(After her.)* Mom. Mom!

               *Slam of door as SARA leaves. She doubles over in
               pain. Black.*

Scene 18
Glen Abbey Golf Course.

               *At the practice tee, waiting to be called. SAM comes
               on.*

SAM: *(Entering.)* Tee off's another five minutes.

RON: That's OK.

               A few practice swings perfectly executed by both.

               So this is a new job?

SAM: Yeah, they hired me just before the election.

RON: What'd you do before—same kind of thing?

SAM: More or less, yeah. I was with Greenpeace.

RON: That's a leap from that—to this.

SAM: Somewhat.

RON: You enjoy Greenpeace?

SAM: It was a blast. I went to work for them right out of
               university—I was an Ecology Major. Our last
               campaign was that expressway in Hamilton.

RON: That was you organizing those demos?

SAM: Sorry.

RON: You caused us a lot of grief. That stunt with the Raging Grannies handcuffed across the ravine—that went worldwide.

SAM: My finest hour.

RON: If you hadn't lost the keys.

SAM: Yeah.

RON: So what's with the switch to education?

SAM: We lost the expressway fight.

RON: There's lots of other environmental battles going on—the moraine, the airport expansion, the

SAM: - I needed a better paying gig. I bought a house. We.

RON: You married?

SAM: Yeah. To Steve. I'm gay. We're gay. I guess that's obvious. If I am, Steve, he's going to be too.

RON: He could be straight and very surprised. Although, with that shirt... I know you have to earn your salary at some point this morning, so let's get it over with right now so we can enjoy the game. I cannot see my Ministry ever paying for private schools. Period.

SAM: We don't want funding—we want equality.

RON: Who exactly do you want equality with?

SAM: The Catholics.

RON: The Catholics are a constitutional anomaly. Among other things.

SAM: The Catholics are funded.

RON: And you want to be funded too. Equality can get very expensive.

SAM: But why should a Catholic school be more fundable than, say, an Islamic one?

RON: Logically, it's not. But there's the matter of the BNA Act. We wouldn't have a Canada if we hadn't given the Catholics their own schools. And to be quite honest, there's a helluva lot more Catholics than Muslims.

SAM: We'd settle for tax breaks restored.

RON: Tax breaks are the thin edge of a very pricey wedge.

SAM: The Charter of Rights

RON: - Oh stop, Sam. You're not going to throw the Charter at me, are you? Out here?

SAM: You love the Charter!

RON: Not on a Saturday morning at Glen Abbey

SAM: - You're famous for using it! Man, when you used it to defend that girl who wanted to walk around topless on hot days—that was brilliant. And the bluegrass singer who was putting posters up on utility poles—on the surface it seemed trivial, but it's been cited in just about every freedom of speech case ever since

RON: - The singer and the jiggler. My legacy.

SAM: And the Holocaust denier. You defended him with the Charter too.

RON: That's the one I want to forget.

SAM: But you were right. Sure, he was slime, but if saying disgusting things is illegal, well, we'd all be in jail by now.

RON: *(Pause.)* My parents disowned me over that case. And lately I've been thinking maybe they were right. Have you seen that bastard's website?

SAM: You couldn't have known that then. There wasn't

even an internet when you took that case. *(Beat.)* I'm sorry about your parents.

RON: I've reconciled with my mother. My Dad died before we could patch things up. OK, Sam, be straight with me, excuse the pun. When can I expect a bunch of raging evangelical grannies to be handcuffed to my office furniture?

SAM: We're a lot broader-based than that. And the Foundation is too—sophisticated—to do anything fun.

RON: Just as well. Barbara would make mincemeat of them. As a matter of fact, I'm half surprised she hasn't shown up to chaperone me. I left my cell in my locker, on purpose. We'd better get to the tee. *(Moving off.)* Hey—didn't Greenpeace try to stop that golf course on the escarpment? Where did you stand on that?

Scene 19
Ron's office.

                The phone rings.

BARBARA: Rankin.

                Light up on SARA.

SARA: Do you know where Ron is? He's not answering.

BARBARA: Hi Sara. He's out golfing. He's probably turned his cell off. It's not you he's avoiding, it's me.

SARA: Do you know which course?

BARBARA: Glen Abbey.

SARA: Glen Abbey! Did he say what he's doing after?

BARBARA: He's driving up to Ashburnham—he's cutting the ribbon at the new Golden Plough Lodge at uh 3:30.

SARA: *(Beat.)* If he calls—tell him—tell him we've got a bit of trouble here. It's Marc.

BARBARA: Anything I can do?

SARA: No, thank you.

BARBARA: I can phone Glen Abbey and get him paged or

SARA: - No, let him enjoy his game. I've left him messages —I'm assuming he'll re-establish contact with the outside world at the 19th hole.

Scene 20
The 19th hole.

                       SAM and RON have drinks.

RON: I've got to say, for a reformed tree hugger, you're a hell of a golfer.

SAM: You smoked me!

RON: I'm a bit of a ringer.

SAM: Your bio said you were quite the hotshot.

RON: Ashburnham Golf and Country Club. It's a Stanley Thompson course—

SAM: Really?

RON: My Dad played there. He had to threaten his way in—no Jews allowed. It was a private club. Now gosh—why does that ring a bell?

SAM: *(Laughs.)* We're inclusive.

RON: I can't quite see a Muslim kid wanting to go to Holy Blood of Christ Secondary.

SAM: Seriously, wouldn't it be more consistent, given your belief in the Charter, to want to give everyone the same access to the school of their choice? Isn't that just being fair?

RON: Where is the greater good served? By allowing everyone equal access to the schools of their choice—or maintaining a high quality system that is equally open to everyone?

SAM: You couldn't wait to golf here.

RON: Leave golf out of it. Besides anyone can belong to this place if they have enough money...maybe I'm talking myself into a corner

SAM: This is a private club—the best in the country.

RON: Choice and quality don't have to be an either/or situation. But the bottom line is—you represent over a hundred groups. Every penny we give you— or every tax dollar you deduct—is money we can't feed into the public system. And the Harris government already stripped the public schools— so it could give tax breaks to the Premier's golf buddies—damn, there's golf again

SAM: - Most of the members of the Foundation aren't wealthy. If they don't get the tax credits, they can't run their schools—and that's denying people the right to be educated in the way they want

RON: - We're going to have to agree to disagree. Now, let me pay my half of the greens fees.

SAM: It's on me.

RON: You told me you can't even afford to fix your own roof.

SAM: I can't afford to putt in my own backyard. I should've said, 'It's on us.'

RON: As in the Foundation. Out of curiosity, who's the member here? No names, just tell me which faction—Christian, Jewish, Muslim

SAM: - Rich and WASP.

RON: Ahh, the cabal's silent partner. The one it's toughest to find the moral high ground for.

His phone rings.

And right on cue. It's Barbara. *(Answers.)* Hello.

Light up on BARBARA.

BARBARA: Sara's been trying to get you. Don't you check your messages? Marc's in trouble.

RON: Marc? What kind of trouble?

BARBARA: I don't know. But she wants you home.

RON: I'm on my way.

Light off BARBARA.

I've got to go.

Pulls out money.

Let me at least get the drinks. We can't have your Christian and Muslim pals paying for booze. *(Stops. Softens.)* Listen, I enjoyed the game. Maybe we can have a rematch at Ashburnham sometime.

RON exits, dialing SARA on his cell as he leaves. SAM sits for a second, then dials his own cell.

SAM: Steve? I think I blew it. I had to argue with him. Get the last word in. I don't do that with you, do I? Well, if I do, it's likely for a reason. Christ. I just did it again. Why don't you meet me at Woody's in an hour? Let's skip the yardwork today, please? Can't we mulch tomorrow? Right now I just want to drink.

Scene 21
Ron's house—upstairs and downstairs.

MARC and ZIMRAN are coming through the basement window.

ZIMRAN: Do you always enter your house this way?

MARC: I do if my parents are upstairs and on the warpath.

They're in. ZIMRAN hands over the knapsack.

Thanks man. You saved my ass.

ZIMRAN: But they still arrested you.

MARC: I forgot I had some E on me. But if they'd got their hands on this—did you look?

ZIMRAN: Yes. Sorry.

MARC: The cops still have your knapsack. I'll get it back—I can say I need it for school. I hope there wasn't anything valuable in it.

ZIMRAN: Just my biology notes.

MARC: You can have mine.

They laugh. "As if."

ZIMRAN: Is this your room?

MARC: Yeah. I used to sleep upstairs but this is better—I can come and go whenever I want. That window's always open. Listen, if your father ever gets on your case, and you need to get the hell out—seriously. You're welcome here.

ZIMRAN: Won't your parents

MARC: - They hardly ever come down here, Dad never does—even if they did and you were here, they'd be OK with that. They'd get all fuzzy and liberal.

ZIMRAN: But I cannot offer you the same refuge.

MARC: That's OK.

ZIMRAN: It is not OK. *(Beat.)* Are you going to jail?

MARC: Naw. Dad got me off. I'll get a lecture or something.

Focus back upstairs.

RON: I can only do that once. And believe me, it really went against the grain.

SARA: Was I right to leave him in overnight?

RON: Absolutely. Maybe that's all he needs. *(Beat.)* Who are we kidding? Where is he anyway?

SARA: Downstairs I think. He's got a Malach friend coming over.

RON: Really?

SARA: That's what he said.

RON: He's hanging out with Malachs?

SARA: It explains why there was a Malach Bible in his knapsack. He switched packs.

RON: But Malachs don't do—*(Pause.)* Maybe this was an isolated incident.

SARA: No. He's been skipping half his classes. He was forging notes on your letterhead.

RON: What else?

SARA: I um—I—I'm starting to get a little afraid of him.

RON: How do you mean?

SARA: Physically.

RON: Has he hit you?

SARA: No, not hit. Pushed. *(Over RON's reaction:)* There's a line, you know, a line between being a teenager or even a bad teenager and something else and he's just kind of on it, Ron, or just about to step over it and I can't handle him, the school certainly can't handle him, Jesus they can't even tell if he's in class or not and

RON: - What're you saying? Should I quit politics?

SARA: No! No. That's not the solution.

RON:	Because I will if that's what it takes, I'll quit and come back here
SARA:	- It's gone further than that.
	Pause.
RON:	You're thinking something.
SARA:	Yes.
RON:	What.
SARA:	I've been asking around—making inquiries. *(Beat.)* You're not going to like this… Better get us drinks—
	Light off them and back on MARC and ZIMRAN.
MARC:	They've gone quiet. That could be a bad sign.
ZIMRAN:	Will he beat you?
MARC:	No. Why would you ask that—does your old man?
ZIMRAN:	*(Pause.)* Sometimes.
MARC:	What for? Doing your homework? What the hell do you do wrong?
ZIMRAN:	Disrespect.
MARC:	Would he beat you if he knew you were here?
ZIMRAN:	No. We are not supposed to mix with you, but of course you are our customers, and we are—grateful of course for you bringing us here—my father understands that, and he knows that your father is—powerful—and where we came from, we were too isolated, we were not connected, so he wouldn't be upset
MARC:	- But if he knew you'd been hiding a knapsack of dope at the store…
ZIMRAN:	He would do aerobics on my head. But listen, my friend—I have to go. I have a—uh—presentation

tomorrow, at school. Hey. *(He saw this in a sneaked-in TV moment:)* Don't get up. I can let myself out.

MARC:　　Asshole.

　　　　　ZIMRAN looks stricken.

　　　　　No, I mean that, that's a good thing.

ZIMRAN:　There are good assholes?

MARC:　　There are good friends.

ZIMRAN:　A good friend who is also an asshole?

　　　　　He does handshake with MARC. Black on them. Lights on RON and SARA.

RON:　　So what's your idea?

SARA:　　Pine Grove Academy.

RON:　　What's that.

SARA:　　It's a boarding school, halfway between here and Ottawa.

RON:　　Pine Grove "Academy"?

SARA:　　It's one of those tough places.

RON:　　Sounds like a boot camp.

SARA:　　Yeah, that's pretty accurate.

RON:　　Come on Sara—Marc in a boot camp?

SARA:　　How about Marc in reform school?

RON:　　*(Pause.)* OK. Tell me more.

SARA:　　There are just forty boys. Ten instructors.

RON:　　I kind of prefer 'teachers'.

SARA:　　They have classes all morning and the rest of the day is physical activity. One of the things they do is work a small farm.

RON:	There's a skill he'll need. What's the rub?
SARA:	The obvious one—the school's private.
RON:	*(Pause.)* I'd guessed that.
SARA:	Well, the optics are terrible.
RON:	Fuck the optics.
SARA:	There's nothing like it in the public system. I looked all over to see if there was some place with extra discipline
RON:	- At this Pine Grove—they don't do anything to the kids, do they? I've heard of some—military ones. They can be brutal.
SARA:	There's no physical discipline whatsoever. It's in their Charter.
RON:	No one touches Marc.
SARA:	They do have a harsh regimen though of uh mental conditioning. It's not brainwashing but in their literature
RON:	- You're not a hundred per cent on side with this are you?
SARA:	There's no parental visitation.
RON:	All year?
SARA:	He gets a weekend home after three months.
RON:	It's like we're the problem!
SARA:	We are.
RON:	I should quit.
SARA:	And resent him forever? Not now, not when you're in a position to do so much good… Besides, honey— it's too late for quitting, way too late.
RON:	How much is this joint?

SARA: Tuition's forty thousand.

RON: WHAT!

SARA: We can afford it. The station is minting money. And if it works?

RON: Forty thousand. Wow.

SARA: The money part's easy. What do you think?

RON: *(Beat.)* OK.

SARA: OK.

RON: But let's do it before I have second thoughts. What?!

SARA: There's another problem.

RON: What.

SARA: Getting him in.

RON: He sounds like the ideal candidate.

SARA: There's a waiting list.

RON: How long?

SARA: Two years.

RON: We can't wait two years.

SARA: We have to jump the line.

RON: OK. There's really no other school.

SARA: Nothing approaching this one. Trust me.

RON: *(Pause.)* I can swing it.

> *They are in each other's arms.*

SARA: He's a good kid, under all that bullshit. I know it. Sometimes I look at him and I can still see you. We'll get him back.

RON: I'd like to talk to him.

SARA:	About going to Pine Grove? It's not allowed. Apparently the introduction to the school is— supposed to be abrupt. They uh oh God they grab you out of your home environment
RON:	- What, like an abduction?
SARA:	Yes.
RON:	Oh man.

Pause.

I'm still going to try and reach him.

SARA:	OK, but don't tell him about

MARC has entered during the last.

Marc, we were just

MARC:	- You were just talking about me?
RON:	Sit down.
MARC:	I'm on my way out.
RON:	No you're not. Sit down. SIT DOWN!

MARC sits, apart from RON, and almost immediately begins tuning him out.

This has gone on long enough. Everything. Your mother and I have been turning a blind eye and that was a big mistake, clearly. Trusting you. Letting you have your own space. Giving you a generous allowance. Expecting you would actually attend classes like any other normal fifteen year-old.

Light begins fading on MARC.

And in return, we are asking for very little: a modicum of civility and—oh, the imposition—the expectation that you would behave in a reasonably respectable, law-abiding fashion and not embarrass us with criminal behaviour.

By now, MARC is out of the light.

I don't know exactly how we've screwed up so badly, but we have, and the time has come to pay the piper. Marc. Marc?

RON pulls out his cell phone, as light goes off him.

Scene 22
Sam's house.

SAM has a drink in one hand. His cell rings.

SAM: Hello? No—no problem. I was just doing some—plumbing. I can meet you anywhere—you're up in Ashburnham—you want me to drive up there? No? Okay, then—your office in three hours. No problem, sir. Ron. *(Hangs up.)* Shit.

Scene 23
Ron's office.

Three hours later.

BARBARA: *(Entering.)* You're back. Lordy, do we need to talk.

RON: I know.

BARBARA: Who first.

RON: Shoot.

BARBARA: I just heard from my friend in the Premier's office. He's cancelling that expressway in Hamilton today. *(Beat.)* And he knows about Marc.

RON: Brilliant.

BARBARA: I told my friend to reassure him—it's not going to be in the press; Marc's a juvenile, your wife owns half the local media…

RON: He must know I leaned on the cops.

BARBARA: Yup. And that's what's really pissing him off. If that gets out... What were you thinking?

RON: I know it's wrong. And if I have to quit over it, I will... All I can say is, if you saw your son sitting in a jail cell, you'd do the same damn thing. I am an idealistic man

BARBARA: - Yes and

RON: - But I'm not stupidly idealistic. Not anymore. Losing my Dad over a court case I didn't really need to take on except that I was—idealistic—that was—well, I learned. Marc is at risk. It's not going to get into the press; I don't see them picking this up, they pretty much leave politicians' kids alone.

BARBARA: Except the Premier's daughter

RON: - She's twenty-four and she drove a bloody government limo into the side of a bar. Marc's a kid, a minor. They're going to cut me some slack. This business is brutal on the kids. We're going to put him in a boarding school. It's not negotiable, Barbara. Some people might say it's hypocritical. I don't give a fuck.

SAM knocks, enters.

SAM: There was no one out there.

BARBARA: We're in a meeting and you don't have an appointment.

RON: Actually he does. Thank you Barbara for— understanding.

BARBARA doesn't leave.

Thank you?

BARBARA leaves. SAM watches her go; maybe makes an indication to effect of "She doesn't like me, does she."

SAM:　　　I'm sorry—I overstepped myself before. I really meant it to be a friendly game of golf

RON:　　　- I like a good debate. Sam, thanks for coming down on such short notice. I'll get to the point. Please (sit down). I'm having trouble with my son.

SAM:　　　I'm sorry to hear that

RON:　　　- I don't understand it all, the why of it—but he's—out of control, Sara and I are scared shitless, I wouldn't be telling you this except... He's been picked up for drugs, selling. We—we think he needs a more regulated environment.

SAM:　　　Uh huh.

RON:　　　A different school.

SAM:　　　OK.

RON:　　　He needs a place like Pine Grove Academy. Do you know it?

SAM:　　　Pine Grove's a member of the Foundation.

RON:　　　Yeah, I knew that.

SAM:　　　They have an incredible track record. But sir, Ron—the Minister of Education sending his

RON:　　　- If it takes a private school to save my son, so be it.

SAM:　　　Of course.

RON:　　　*(Pause.)* There's a waiting list.

SAM:　　　I'll make the call.

> *RON starts to thank him.*

No—don't thank me. I'm glad to—do something useful.

RON:　　　I can't promise any quid pro quo

SAM: - Nor should you. The foundations won't hear any
                of this from me. They're going to find out, you know
                that—just not from me.

Scene 24
Principal's office.

> *ZIMRAN has more confidence. This time there is no
> "letter" being read from. His iPod or earphones
> might be visible.*

ZIMRAN: I wish to speak to you about two classes. Health and
                Biology. Malachs do not believe in Evolution. My
                Biology teacher says it is good science and maybe
                that is true, he is a wise man who is well-educated,
                but that does not change the fact it is heresy. Surely
                it is against my rights to force me to listen to heresy?
                And in Health, we are taught methods of birth
                control. The kinds of diseases people get while
                having sex. Why homosexuality is enjoyable. How
                to abort a fetus. None of these practices occur in our
                community and, as the senior Malach student, it is
                my duty to speak out about this now, before anyone
                else is exposed.

Scene 25
In Ron's car.

> *RON, SARA and MARC are in the car. MARC is
> listening to music and oblivious to SARA and RON.*

RON: They aren't here.

SARA: They said noon.

RON: They just show up and grab him?

SARA: Yes.

RON: Yeah, well if they can't even meet us on time

SARA: - We're two minutes early

RON: - They should have been waiting. We have to say something to him.

SARA: They said not to tell him.

RON: He thinks we're going to the cottage.

SARA: It's their process.

MARC: *(Taking off earphones.)* How come you pulled over?

RON: Dammit Sara, I'm telling him

SARA: - Ron don't

MARC: Tell me what.

RON: Marc, we aren't going to the cottage.

MARC: So where are we going?

RON: Your Mom and I

SARA: - Ron

RON: No, we're telling him!

               RON and SARA face forward during this, too ashamed to look at their son.

               Son. Sometimes parents, sometimes people have to do things they think are in the best interest

MARC: *(Putting earphones back on.)*—Oh Jesus, another lecture.

SARA: It's not a lecture. Listen to your father.

RON: Your mother and I have decided—we aren't doing this lightly, we lost a lot of sleep over this but we think it's right

SARA: - This has been the most difficult decision

RON: - I—we—want you to know that we love you

SARA: - We really love you

RON: - We love you and that's why we're doing this. I know I haven't said that enough

> *MARC has noticed something, he takes earphones back off.*

MARC: - Whoah—that's weird. Who're they?

SARA: Those guys are the

MARC: - Someone's pulled up behind us. Dad—Dad, I think we should get going—Dad, they're getting out of their van, Dad. Dad? Dad!? What's going on? Dad! DAD!

> *Black.*

> *End of Act One.*

Act Two

Scene 1
The 'Breakfast with Sara' set. Now.

> *BARBARA is winding up what appears to have been an extended monologue, with SARA fidgeting, listening anxiously, periodically trying to interject.*

BARBARA: ...And then I moved to Toronto, all my belongings jammed into one cardboard suitcase—but because of that Lions Club scholarship and the student grants they had in those days, I was able to attend the University of Toronto. The first of my family to go past Grade Ten. So there's little dirty-kneed Barbara Rankin, sitting in front of profs like Northrop Frye and Marshall McLuhan. Well, Frye. I couldn't get into McLuhan's class and wouldn't have understood him if I had. I got my Honours BA and, after graduation, I went into the public service—I just crossed the road and started working at Queens Park. I bounced around a few ministries and eventually ended up as Executive Assistant

SARA: *(Soto.)*—Your point

BARBARA: - My point is: it's a long, long way from Plevna to the Ministry of Education, and a lot of very good people and organizations gave me a hand along the way. I'm proud of how hard I've worked. But that and all the generous folk in the world don't amount to a hill of beans without a strong public system backing me up

SARA: - And gosh—we're out of time. That's it for 'Breakfast with Sara'—we've been talking with Barbara Rankin, who is the Executive Assistant

BARBARA: - Former

SARA: - Former Executive Assistant in the Education Ministry and the woman who is spearheading the library campaign in the lovely village of Plevna. We'll see you tomorrow, it's antiques day on 'Breakfast with Sara' so come on up to the studio and let our experts assess your family jewels.

BILL: And cut.

SARA: Jesus.

BILL: What should I do for the next half hour?

SARA: Can you rerun yesterday's interview?

BARBARA: I thought we were going to have a cheque ceremony.

SARA: We were, until you decided to waste twenty minutes talking about yourself!

BARBARA: You told me to!

SARA: I also asked you to talk about Ron. And stupidly, I'd hoped you could keep off the schools thing, no one wants to hear about your bloody teacher. "She was so beautiful." God. *(Leaving.)* You know, I thought that—no matter how pissed off you were—over one issue—that you would at least choke back your bile and come on here and

BARBARA: – Talk about how wonderful and principled your husband is?

SARA: *(To BILL.)* I'm going to be at the golf club if you need me. My husband and son are having a friendly game and I'm going to go join them—whack a few balls. *(Leaving.)* The library will get its bloody cheque. But Ron's going up there and presenting it, not you.

BARBARA: Can he even find the place?

SARA: You know, Ron trusted you. We both thought that
             we could count on—well, if not your loyalty—at
             least your co-operation. I'm out of here.

             SARA exits.

BARBARA: *(To BILL.)* I don't think I relaxed her.

BILL: She's always jumpy at election time. You should
             have seen her during the last one, when things were
             so tight. Hey—the PSA—you still want to record it?

BARBARA: You bet your sweet bippy I do. Could I come back
             next week? I need to work up my speech a bit with
             my uh assistant. Make sure I have my facts correct.
             Because, as the lady said at the start of the show—
             it's been quite the journey… these past few
             months…

Scene 2
Ron's office and a pay phone in the country.

             *Seguing back in time, as in the first act. BARBARA
             enters RON's area.*

BARBARA: Your son is holding on line two.

RON: I know.

BARBARA: Aren't you going to take it?

RON: Tell him I'm in a meeting. I'm not supposed to talk
             to him, OK? Those are the rules. Please.

BARBARA: But he sounds

RON: - Don't make this any harder.

             *BARBARA uses the phone on RON's desk. Light on
             MARC, at a payphone somewhere. Likely a village
             store or gas station.*

BARBARA: Marc?

MARC: Yes?

BARBARA: I'm afraid I just missed him. Sorry, my fault. Can
             you call back?

MARC: No.

BARBARA: Is there a message?

MARC: Tell him I've learned my lesson. Tell him I want to
             come home.

             MARC hangs up; lights off him.

RON: I don't want to talk about it. I don't want a lecture.

BARBARA: He wants to come home.

RON: He knows the rules. He's allowed a two-day visit in
             a few weeks, if they think he has made progress.

BARBARA: Does he know that?

RON: Yes. He also knows he's not supposed to be calling.
             The rules are: no contact with the family for the first
             three months. Nothing. That's the second time he's
             managed to get to a phone. Which suggests he
             hasn't reformed.

BARBARA: If it makes any difference, he's been very polite both
             times.

             Pause.

RON: What?!

BARBARA: My source in the Premier's office—they know about
             the school.

RON: God, apparently you can't even burp in this
             province without your source finding out. Who is
             this bloody friend? She should be killed. The press is
             not going to use this.

BARBARA: Unless they think someone else is. Do you really
             think your golf buddy is going to be able to hold off
             manipulating this?

RON: Actually, yes. Hard though this may be for you to imagine—I think we have an ethical lobbyist on our hands. Sam hasn't asked for a thing. I don't think he's going to. I'm sorry you don't agree with what we've done.

BARBARA: I didn't say that. With my nephews and nieces—I'd toss aside any number of—rules. *(Looking at daytimer or Blackberry.)* Tomorrow. You're in Ashburnham during the day: one funeral, then a church bazaar, you're handing out trophies at the girls' soccer finals and then you have to go north for a monster truck demolition derby tractor pull

RON: - Oh man.

BARBARA: I know. But you need to hook up with the rural voters.

RON: There's really going to be a bunch of cars driving over each other?

BARBARA: It'll be cathartic. You can pretend they're Tories.

Scene 3
Zimran's store.

> *The phone rings. ZIMRAN has his harq off, and is maybe wearing a do-rag. Maybe doing a couple of dance steps while watching a video—and not doing it too badly.*

ZIMRAN: Vettur Electronics, Zimran speaking.

MARC: Hey.

ZIMRAN: Hello?

MARC: Hey, it's me. Marc.

ZIMRAN: Marc! Where are you?

MARC: Can you talk? Where's your Dad?

ZIMRAN:	He is up in Toronto getting new things we can sell to others but never use ourselves. It is just me here.
MARC:	No customers?
ZIMRAN:	We are closed. I am supposed to be doing inventory.
MARC:	Zimran, you've got to help me. Can you get a car? Or, or—if I hitchhike, can you get me a place, is there somewhere I can stay—You've got to get me out of here.
ZIMRAN:	How far away is it?
MARC:	It's two hours up Highway 7. Maybe just an hour and a half. If I know when you're coming I can get out to the highway and—Zimran?
ZIMRAN:	*(Pause.)* I will try something. Perhaps I can get the van. I can say I have to make a customer delivery. But how do I get in touch with you?
MARC:	I'll call back and arrange a time. I've gotta go.

> *Light off MARC. ZIMRAN continues with his dancing. He might repeat some hip hop lines. And then he turns around and freezes.*

ZIMRAN:	Father. You are back. *(Shows fear, backs up, hands up to ward off a blow.)* Father!

> *Black on ZIMRAN.*

Scene 4
Sam is at Woody's again.

> *SAM's cell rings. He gets it out.*

SAM:	*(Looks at call display.)* Shit. *(To his friends.)* Sorry, I have to take this, keep it down, it's my boss. *(Moves off a bit.)* Reverend Fulton. Yes. This is late—where am I? Home! Oh that's the neighbours, yeah, they're playing music again. Sorry. *(Moves to a quieter area.)* Is this better? Yes sir. You were talking to the

Premier? He just called you? (*Pause.*) Pine Grove. No. I didn't tell you. I didn't think it was relevant. I was just helping him—he was in a jam, I knew you'd hear, obviously Pine Grove'd inform you, I just didn't see how it was germane... (*Pause.*) The Premier's doing what?! No, I am surprised, I uh— no one's told me any of this—of course, it makes sense they'd call you first, sure—I'll go home and check my e-mails. I mean, I am home, (*Mouths: "Fuck."*) There's going to be—Monday afternoon, press conference, yes, I'll be there, sure. That's really great news, Reverend. Yes, a real uh step forward. OK. Bye. (*Hangs up.*) Yeah, a real giant fucking step for mankind.

> *Black on SAM.*

Scene 5
Ron's car.

> *Evening. RON and SARA are headed to the demolition derby.*

SARA: I'm looking forward to this.

RON: Liar.

SARA: Barbara's right. It's a whole new crop of voters.

RON: I get nervous the second I cross the IQ line.

SARA: Ronnnn.

RON: I'm not driving any demolition cars.

SARA: They won't ask you. Maybe they'll ask me—I'm better known up here than you are.

RON: Good. You do it.

SARA: I just might.

RON: Wear a helmet. I need your brains.

SARA: Just my brains?

RON: What do you think.

                 Phone rings. SARA looks.

SARA: It's yours. Unknown number. Hello? *(Listens for a second.)* No, it's not Barbara, it's Sara. Sara, the wife? *(Laughs.)* He's right here. He's driving—I'll put you on hands free. We're on our way to a demolition derby and we should limit the crashes to when we get there. It's the Premier.

PREMIER: *(Voice is treated.)* Demolition derby eh.

RON: Yeah.

PREMIER: I envy you. Those derbies are a lot of fun. I think my daughter's in training for one. Listen. The new poll's in, it looks good, real promising. Nothing like a few French-speaking nurses and a cancelled expressway to put the electorate in a loving mood. We've got one more announcement to make Monday and then we're good to go.

RON: "Good to go"?

PREMIER: Gentlemen: drop your writs. I'm smelling blood, Ronny. Torrrry blood.

RON: This soon?

PREMIER: Yup.

RON: And the announcement you're making?

PREMIER: After you get your fill of the monster trucks, we need you back here, my people are going to brief you on the spin, there's a uh slight element of uh spinning involved, actually there's a whole lot of spinning to be done. But you shouldn't have any problem with that, apparently.

RON: What's that mean?

PREMIER: Two words, Ron. 'Pine Grove.' Or is that one word.

RON:	*(Pause.)* Are you going to tell me what this is about?
PREMIER:	Not over the phone. This is face to face stuff. Now go smash 'em up, pretend they're Tories.

PREMIER hangs up.

RON:	What do you think the announcement is?
SARA:	Obviously something to do with your Ministry.
RON:	He's going to toss a bone to the private schools.
SARA:	Without consulting you?
RON:	I'm just the Minister, Sara. The Premier's office is driving the policy right now, if you can call this policy. Ohhh man.

And then the cell rings again.

SARA:	It's Barbara.
RON:	No. Not now. No. She's heard obviously. You can't—burp in this province without that woman hearing. Isn't she supposed to be up in Plevna dedicating her library? Maybe that's next week. Let it ring.
SARA:	You really think they're going to
RON:	- Tax credits, I bet.
SARA:	But that's outrageous!
RON:	And I'm the guy who's announcing it.
SARA:	*(Beat.)* Can you?
RON:	Put it this way—if I can't, I'm going to have to resign.
SARA:	*(Pause.)* This is going to sound like the understatement of the century.
RON:	Shoot.

SARA: Politicians have changed their minds before.

RON: This one hasn't.

SARA: *(Pause.)* If we're going to be honest, I think you already did change your mind.

RON: What do you mean?

SARA: When we sent Marc to Pine Grove. We didn't have to deal with the implications—philosophically—not really, because we knew we'd never have to justify it in public and, in private—Ron, you know it was our only choice.

RON: Because we were fuck-ups.

SARA: We had no choice. Now, you have no choice, unless you want to give it all up. And, in the process, hand the province back to the Tories. So let's do what has to be done. Ron, it's not a big change for us. It's not. Maybe not even philosophically. There are rights arguments you can use to justify it. You know that. We can do this. It's not a leap. It's just a 'shift.' We're liberals. We can shift.

Scene 6
Press Gallery and Woody's.

               We go directly to the Monday afternoon press conference. RON has turned from the car seat, and is making the announcement, with apparent conviction.

RON: ...And so, after a great deal of deliberation, the government has decided to restore the tax credit for independent schools. In addition, we will be establishing a Crown Commission

               This begins moving to a TV monitor at Woody's. SAM is watching with a drink.

               to investigate our current funding models for

schools in both the public and private sectors. This constitutes an acknowledgement on the part of your government of the growing cultural and social diversity of this province and the need to accommodate everyone under a welcoming fabric

BARBARA enters the bar.

BARBARA: - You must be very proud of yourself.

SAM: Oh Jesus.

BARBARA: What'd you do, blackmail him?

SAM: I beg your pardon?

BARBARA: You got his son into Pine Grove; is this the payback?

SAM: It'd be a pretty big one. How'd you even find me here?

BARBARA: You told me it was your local. And I called your house. Your roommate says to get your butt home and do a few pints of housework.

SAM: Buzz off.

BARBARA: I think I'll have a beer first. I want to know everything you know. For starters, how come you're looking so miserable? You just won. Isn't the Foundation having a wild celebration right now?

SAM: I'm not missing any party. The Muslims and Christians don't drink the Jews' wine. The Jews won't eat the Christians' food. And the rich guys don't want any of them in their club.

BARBARA: Or maybe they just didn't invite you.

SAM: Would you please go.

BARBARA: Not until you tell me what happened.

SAM: Would it surprise you to know that I don't know what the hell happened? I got a phone call from the head of the Foundation, Saturday night. Reverend

Fulton told me he heard direct from the Premier. I didn't know a thing about it—OK? The decision was made in the Premier's office. In other words—your man's clean. He didn't have anything to do with it either.

BARBARA: He's up there announcing it.

SAM: He's the bloody Minister of Education, it's his job.

BARBARA: He doesn't favour private schools.

SAM: So what do you expect him to do—resign? Oh shit, you do. You want him to fall on his sword.

BARBARA: What're you drinking?

SAM: I have no idea.

BARBARA: It looks good. *(At bartender.)* Hey!

SAM: You do realize this is a gay bar.

BARBARA: So?

SAM: Duhh.

BARBARA: Duhh. Maybe I'm gay.

SAM: Even a dyke wouldn't wear plaid and stripes.

BARBARA: Well, I'm thirsty. The bartender's ignoring me. Hey you with the shirt off! Shake your bony ass and get me one of those.

SAM: Oh man, this day just keeps getting better and better

BARBARA: - I believe you didn't bribe Ron. I almost wish you had.

SAM: You might be more loyal to your employer, you know. In the world of politicians he's pretty much up there at the top. And if you ever thought he'd change his mind because of something I did—the most pathetic lobbyist in the province…

BARBARA: He's ignoring me. HEY!

SAM: Anyway, you should be happy for him. This is
            going to save his seat—it's going to win him a whole
            pile of Christian Heritage votes... Why do you care
            anyway? Your job is to support him.

BARBARA: Briefly it was more than job. Like working for
            Greenpeace was for you. We're thirsty!!

SAM: Chad, can you—thanks—

BARBARA: Can I ask you something?

SAM: No.

BARBARA: Was there ever a time when you felt comfortable at
            the Foundation? I'm only asking because, why, look
            what I've got here. It's the syllabus for that big
            Islamic school they've built north of the city. Now
            there's something in here about people like you—
            oh gosh, they don't like fags much, do they. Here's
            the Christian high school prospectus, the one
            they're building near Windsor. Hmm. Family
            studies. D'you think that includes teaching about
            children with two Daddies…

SAM: You've made your point

BARBARA: - And the Malachs in my boss's riding. Get a load of
            this. "We need to provide a safe environment for
            our children, far away from the pro-abortion, pro-
            homosexuality, pro-sex teachings of the public
            system."

SAM: - I didn't know this sort of stuff when I took the job.

BARBARA: Oh come on.

SAM: People have the right to teach what they want.

BARBARA: Arguable.

SAM: As long as they aren't teaching hate.

BARBARA: And this isn't hate?

SAM: No.

BARBARA: You sure? Should we do a poll here? Hey everybody!

SAM: - Oh for Christ's sake, have you never made a wrong choice?

BARBARA: (*Softens.*) Yes. I've made lots of wrong choices. I've trusted the wrong people, lots of times. (*Packing stuff up.*) For the record. I don't blame you. You're obviously no happier with this than I am.

SAM: I thought I could take a job I didn't believe in, because I needed the money. OK?

BARBARA: Funny. I didn't need the money and I took a job I actually did believe in. And we've ended up in exactly the same place.

SAM: So what's that make us? A couple of chumps, that's what it makes us.

BARBARA: Yup. (*Pause.*) That guy at your house. Is that your husband?

SAM: Yeah. Steve.

BARBARA: He's really pissed. I'll drive you home.

SAM: I don't want to go home.

BARBARA: (*Beat.*) Then I've got a Plan B.

              No response from SAM.

              Do you want to hear it?

SAM: Uh, no?

BARBARA: Come on.

SAM: What.

BARBARA: I want to show you something. Something that'll stop you crying in your cocktail.

SAM: I like crying in my cocktail.

BARBARA: I've got case of beer in the car, you can drink that
            and cry there

SAM: - I'm not going anywhere

BARBARA: It's either come with me or go home and do
            housework. Housework!? God, is that what you
            people have been fighting for? The right to be dull?
            Now come on. Trust me, this is going to be a lot
            more interesting.

            *Black on BARBARA and SAM, as they get up to
            leave.*

Scene 7
At the bus terminal, early evening.

            *ZIMRAN is standing with his back to the audience.
            His harq is off.*

ZIMRAN: I want a one way ticket. Toronto. When's the next
            bus—what, not until then? There's a red eye?
            What's a red eye? 2 A.M.? OK, I'll take that. Here.

            *Hands over money; turns around; he has been
            injured; perhaps has a bandage on his face. It looks
            self-applied.*

Scene 8
Ron's basement.

            RON and SARA, alone, maybe with drinks.

RON: I managed to avoid Barbara. I thought she'd be at
            the announcement but she must be up north,
            boycotting. She's been leaving plenty of messages
            though. What're we doing down here?

SARA: Wallowing. I come down and pretend he's still
            living with us.

RON: I half expected him to escape from Pine Grove.

SARA: I kind of hoped he would.

RON: God, I can hardly wait to see him. But will he be speaking to us? I've hung up on him three times now.

> *Just then the basement window opens and ZIMRAN begins crawling through.*

What the hell—Marc?

> *He goes over and pulls ZIMRAN down.*

Who the hell are you?!

> *ZIMRAN is shocked—he wasn't expecting anyone. He turns around and starts to leave.*

ZIMRAN: Excuse me. Wrong house.

RON: Wait a minute. *(Pulls him back in.)*

SARA: Zimran?

RON: You know him?

SARA: Are you—Zimran?

ZIMRAN: Yes.

SARA: Marc mentioned you. Let him go, Ron; he's Marc's friend.

RON: How on earth would you guys hook up?

ZIMRAN: At school sir.

RON: Marc was actually there long enough to meet someone?

ZIMRAN: We met during um aerobics. I am sorry to startle you. Marc said I could come here anytime.

RON: Most people come via the door.

ZIMRAN: He told me to use the window. So I would not bother you.

SARA: Marc's been away for nearly two months. You didn't notice?

ZIMRAN: Yes. He called me at the store

SARA notices bandage on ZIMRAN's face.

SARA: - Has someone hit you? Who?

RON: - Listen son, if you were bashed, we need to call the police.

SARA: - Was it a gang? There was that awful thing in the park last year

ZIMRAN: No. It was not a gang. Please do not call the police.

SARA: Was it your father?

RON: Why would you jump to that conclusion?

SARA: You remember the family who stayed with us, the father was a bit

ZIMRAN: - I had taken off my harq. *(When SARA and RON don't seem to get why that was bad:)* And I was wearing a do-rag.

RON: A what?

SARA: You know. *(Motions to her head.)* Marc wears one sometimes.

ZIMRAN: Marc gave one to me. I was wearing it and listening to music. And, dancing, a bit. My father caught me and now I have left home.

RON: Oh.

SARA: But

ZIMRAN: - The next bus to Toronto isn't until 2 A.M. The red eye. That is the overnight bus. I hoped to stay here until then. It is too cold to stay in the park. I do not know anyone else in Ashburnham except other Malachs and they would all report me to my father. Marc said I could stay here if I ever needed to.

SARA: I'm glad you did. Your father should not be hitting you.

RON: What on earth will you do in Toronto?

ZIMRAN: I can get a job in a store. I have always worked in my father's store, so I have experience.

RON: How old are you?

ZIMRAN: Seventeen.

RON: Well. You're an adult. You can decide things for yourself. Why don't you stay overnight. It's stupid to arrive in Toronto in the middle of the night—stay here, you're a lot safer. Sara, can you look at that *(The wound)?* Zimran, this is kind of an awkward situation you've put us in. Your father will be worrying about where you are. He should be told

SARA: - He's come to us. If he doesn't want his father to know we should respect that.

RON: OK. But Zimran, if you stay here, will you promise not to take off? There's lots of buses to Toronto tomorrow—will you stay long enough to at least talk things over with us?

ZIMRAN: Yes. Yes, I can do that. Thank you. Marc said you were kind people.

SARA: He did?

ZIMRAN: He is a kind person himself. I see where he gets that from.

Focus on a somewhat gob-smacked RON and SARA.

Scene 9
Barbara's car and the school library at Plevna.

> *SAM in a car. He's a passenger. Light only on him.*

SAM: *(Gets STEVE.)* Hi honey. Hi. Listen. I'm uh a little delayed. No, I've left Woody's. Um, I might not make it home tonight. Um, well, it's a long story. No no no no no, I'm with a woman. No no no no a real one. I think. Everything's OK honest honest this is a uh job-thing. Yeah. Well. I'm going to Plevna. Plevna. P-L-E—where is Plevna?

> *Light on BARBARA, who is driving.*

BARBARA: North of the jezly IQ line.

SAM: That's Barbara. No no honest, she's an old dyke.

> *BARBARA slugs him.*

A work colleague. I'm just going on a little overnight with her, I'll be back tomorrow morning, I love you. Plevna. Pullevvvna. West of Ottawa. I'll see you tomorrow.

> *Hangs up.*

I'll pay for this, you realize.

BARBARA: It'll be worth it.

SAM: We'll see.

> *Pause.*

BARBARA: And I am impressed.

SAM: With what.

BARBARA: That you came.

SAM: So what are you going to say tonight?

> *Pause; BARBARA might shrug.*

BARBARA: I don't know. I'm terrible at talking in public. I had something all worked up and this morning I was looking it over and it was really dull, I thought I might just wing it, just say how happy I am and cut the stupid ribbon and

SAM: - Oh, you should say something. But nothing formal. It's good to put in some personal stuff.

BARBARA: OK.

SAM: Who's your audience?

BARBARA: The parents. There'll be a lot of kids there too.

SAM: Talk to them. It's their library. Get them to come up front. Like at church. Tell them a story.

BARBARA: Really?

SAM: Yeah. Make it a place you share. A common space.

BARBARA: Oh, you are good.

SAM: I used to be. Is there a story from your childhood? You did have a childhood, didn't you? Tell them about yourself.

BARBARA: But it's pretty standard issue: skinny ugly girl with dirty knees, poor family, nobody'd ever gone past Grade Ten, people made fun of us because our house was small and my brothers were trash and instead of a front yard we had a field of beat-up cars…

SAM: That's a start.

BARBARA: It is? Actually, I could tell them about the day the teacher came by.

SAM: Why was that important?

BARBARA: I was sitting in one of the cars in the yard pretending I was Stirling Moss and I was winning Mosport— Lordy, maybe I am a lesbian.

SAM: You think. Keep going.

BARBARA: Well, suddenly Miss Bailey drove into the yard.
            And you have to understand, I was eight, I idolized
            her. She was always beautifully dressed, compared
            to my mother, she wore earrings, she smelled so
            nice…

> *And now the scene changes to the library. Instead of
> sitting in a car, BARBARA is sitting on a chair,
> talking to the children. Maybe there are balloons
> behind her. SAM watches his new protégé proudly.*

Anyway, I lead her inside—Mom nearly crap—er
has an accident because the house is in its usual
chaos, and suddenly there's this goddess in our
midst, but she sits down in the kitchen with Mom
and says she wants to talk about my education. My
education. In a house where there is not one book
other than the Bible. And this is what she says.
"Your daughter is so smart that if she stays in
school, right through Grade Thirteen, with her
brains she'll get scholarships and provincial grants
for university. I believe she can become a teacher or
a doctor or a lawyer—anything she wants.
Anything." Don't forget: this was the 1950s. A
family for which education was an alien concept. A
dirty-kneed little girl. A teacher-goddess telling a
beaten-down woman that her daughter can escape
her drudgery, can go as far as she wants in life, so far
we don't even know where that farness might be—
it was all there for her. And these books, they might
look like books but they're really magic stepping
stones, and they will lead you from here to
anywhere you want to go. So who wants to help me
cut the ribbon?

> *Black on them.*

Scene 10
Ron's kitchen—the next morning.

SARA and RON.

SARA: We have to send him back.

RON: This is becoming a pattern with us.

SARA: What.

RON: Offloading teenagers. But we shouldn't be harbouring runaways.

SARA: Can we really send him home?

RON: We can't let him go to Toronto. He's completely unequipped for that.

SARA: *(Still a bit in awe.)* He and Marc were friends. That just blows my mind—How they'd ever connect?

RON: - We did sponsor that family. Do you remember how he went out and picked flowers for their room?

SARA: The neighbour's flowers.

RON: Do you think we sold Marc short?

SARA: He was dealing drugs.

RON: And he pushed you. He was out of control. But as far as what to do with Zimran, I don't know. I really don't know. Better get him up.

SARA: Nice to know Malach teenagers sleep in too.

               SARA goes to door and is about to call when ZIMRAN appears.

               Oh. Morning.

ZIMRAN: Good morning.

SARA: Hi—

RON: Morning Zimran

SARA: I've made some breakfast; I got out the recipes I had
                 from when the Vettur family lived with us and…

ZIMRAN: Thank you. I am very hungry. Thinking all night has
                 given me an appetite.

RON: You've got your—back on—does that mean?

ZIMRAN: Yes, sir. I am going to go back home. Running away
                 is not the answer. I belong with my family. It is time
                 for me to suck it up.

RON: "Suck it up"?

ZIMRAN: That's the right phrase isn't it? To take
                 responsibility. I am the son of the community leader
                 and that makes me responsible too.

RON: But son, we're worried for your safety. I would at
                 least like to come with you, talk to your father.

ZIMRAN: - (Points to face.) You're thinking about this. But the
                 important thing is what happens to this. (Touches his
                 heart.) My father is a decent, honourable man and I
                 love him more than anyone in the world. And he has
                 much to teach me. But he is not right all the time,
                 and what I realized last night was there are some
                 things I can teach him now. (Touches bruise.) No, this
                 is not right. It will never happen again, to me or my
                 brothers.

                         Pause.

RON: Wow.

SARA: Zimran, we're very

RON: - I think you're doing the right thing

SARA: - We're very proud of you.

RON: So. Breakfast.

ZIMRAN: Yes. Thank you. I do not want to face my father on
                 an empty stomach.

BARBARA appears at the door.

BARBARA: Anybody home?

SARA: Barbara!

RON: (*Sotto.*) Oh lord.

BARBARA marches in.

BARBARA: I happened to be in the goddamn neighbourhood and I have a few things I'd like to get off my chest

RON: - Barbara, this is our guest, Zimran. Zimran Vettur, Barbara Rankin.

BARBARA: Pleased to meet you. We're just on our way back from Plevna. Sam!

SAM enters.

RON: What the hell's he doing here?

SARA: Who's he?

BARBARA: Right, you haven't met. Sam, this is Sara Munro, Sam Grearson, Zim—

RON: Sam works for the private school folk.

ZIMRAN: Zimran Vettur.

RON: Zimran's a pal of Marc's.

ZIMRAN: Marc is my best friend.

RON: (*Of SAM.*) Did you kidnap him?

BARBARA: Sam and I spent the night together.

RON: Pardon?

BARBARA: In Plevna. Oh, we hardly slept a wink. I had a library to open and then we stayed up all night talking. It's a miracle really. Sam and I started out like two books on uh opposite shelves—but—to stretch the metaphor, we seem to have ended up on the same page.

RON:	*(To BARBARA.)*—OK. I know you're angry. I'm sorry I didn't talk to you before the announcement. I assumed you were in Plevna. And secondly
BARBARA:	- I left about a hundred messages.
SARA:	- This isn't the right time
BARBARA:	I don't see why not.
RON:	Sara's right—we have a guest. OK?
SARA:	Would you like a coffee. Sam? Let's have a coffee and you can tell us how the library opening went.
BARBARA:	Skip the coffee. The opening was lovely. Very moving. I can't work for you now.
RON:	Have you thought that through?
SARA:	This is not the time for this!
BARBARA:	*(Ignoring her.)*—Of course I've thought it through. It's a simple question of 'Can I live with what you've done?' and the answer is an easy simple 'No.'
RON:	*(Pause.)* I'm sorry it's ending like this. *(To ZIMRAN.)* Barbara and I work together at Queens Park, in Toronto
BARBARA:	*(To ZIMRAN.)*—You see, guest, I was all set to retire when Mr. Bloom was made Education Minister. I was going to take my package and go sit by a lake and gently rot. But this man—when he was young, you know what he did? He defended people whose beliefs he didn't agree with, just because he believed they should have the right to have those beliefs. He took stands that were so brave—well, put it this way—have you ever worried about doing something so drastic that your father would never speak to you again?
RON:	OK, stop it now, Barbara
ZIMRAN:	- But I can answer that!

RON: She's not interested in your answer.

BARBARA: You're right. I'm not. I thought, whoah Barbara, here's a new breed of politician, *(Starts breaking down here.)* Barbara, you're a jaded old bureaucrat but this guy's got something worth sticking around for. Principles. And there was one principle in particular, one that has served this country well for a hundred and twenty-five years and made Canada such a great place for so many of us and one that sure saved my life and *(To RON now.)* you've thrown it away so you can kiss the ass of every splinter group in the country.

ZIMRAN: - What's a splinter group?

RON: Malachs are a splinter group.

BARBARA: Muslims, Orthodox Jews…Christians, everyone who wants to separate to

ZIMRAN: - How is it that I'm a splinter—and you aren't?

RON: There's more of her.

SARA: And she was here first.

SAM: There's something else important here too—listen, if we're going to talk about splinter groups. *(To ZIMRAN.)* I'm gay. You're a Malach. He's a Jew. *(Of BARBARA.)* She's a rude, opinionated old bat who can drink me under the table. When you get right down to it, we're all splinters. And none of us split off from each other is worth a damn.

RON: Do you say that in front of your bosses?

SAM: I quit too. First thing this morning I phoned up Reverend Fulton and told him I was finished with the Foundation. I feel fantastic. I'd been avoiding the truth for months. They want their own schools so they can teach their beliefs safely away from the danger of an open classroom. They don't want to hear about people like me. They don't even want to hear about each other. They all just want their own prejudices confirmed

ZIMRAN: - You don't know what it's like to be different.

SAM: Sure I do.

ZIMRAN: Not just different in one area, like being gay. If I look at you, I cannot tell you are gay. But you look at me and know right away I am truly different. Not just about who I choose to have sex with.

> *SAM tries to say "It's not a choice" but is overridden.*

In every belief. You do not know what it is like to sit in a classroom and hear things taught like they are the complete and only truth, and if you do not happen to agree with them, you will fail the class. Or if you ask to be excused you are laughed at... The filth I have been learning is turning me against myself! You talk about separate schools as if they are a bad thing but a Malach school—it would be a good thing, for me.

RON: But son, last night you were all set to run away

ZIMRAN: - I know. The splinter was splintering. And I spent all night thinking about that, and I realized it was wrong.

BARBARA: *(To ZIMRAN.)* Next time you're up all night thinking, ask yourself who your best friend is. And where did you meet him? You met Marc at a public school!

SAM: *(To RON.)* I enjoyed meeting you. Great golf. I'm glad I could help Marc.

RON: Yeah, uh we're very grateful, we'll always be. *(To BARBARA.)* He got Marc in a private school, don't forget.

SAM: *(More to RON.)* If the public system was better

funded there could be schools like Pine Grove. Open to all

BARBARA: -We've said enough, let's get the hell out.

RON: Why don't you?

SARA: - Wait. Barbara, wait. Don't go like this.

              BARBARA turns.

              I know this is going to sound strange, after everything. But—would you come on the show?

BARBARA: Pardon?

SARA: I'm serious. Would you come on 'Breakfast with Sara'?

BARBARA: I hardly think it would be appropriate now.

SARA: Not to talk politics. To talk about the library. You—you've still got a lot of money to raise—we can help with that. I'm serious Barbara. I don't want things to end this way.

BARBARA: Are you buying me off?

RON: Of course she's buying you off. So you better stick to your principles. Say no. Don't worry about all the little Plevnites who'll never get to read a book.

SARA: Ron.

RON: Stick to your goddamn principles, woman. Just keep your noble mouth shut when the Tories win the election next month.

BARBARA: You're no different from them now!

SARA: Ron

RON: You just keep your fucking halo on!

SARA: - You're really not helping.

RON: You've got that fucking halo rammed so tight on your pointy little head you can't think straight!

ZIMRAN: Politics in this country is very exciting.

               This defuses things a bit.

RON: Yes. It's pretty gripping, Zimran. Sorry. Keep the
               halo. Sorry. Barbara, you should do the show, not
               for me, not for her, it'll help the library.

BARBARA: *(Pause.)* All right. OK. I'll come on your show. Sure.
               I'll call you next week—

SARA: We've got to get through Ron's nomination meeting
               on Thursday. Then I'm free.

BARBARA: *(To SAM.)* Ready?

SAM: Let's go.

               *MARC appears at the door. He is well dressed, well-
               groomed. He looks transformed. Perhaps even some
               lighting to accentuate this. The return of the
               prodigal, all spruced up.*

MARC: Hello Mom? Dad?

SARA: Marc?

               Fast black to music, streamers, cheers.

Scene 11
Ron's nomination meeting at the High School.

               *It is a few days later. SARA and RON and MARC
               are in an anteroom off the gym. Cheering offstage.*

SARA: Where is he?

               MARC enters.

               Oh, there you are.

MARC: Sorry—I was talking with some people.

RON: That's OK, son. God—you look like a young
               Conservative in that jacket—you trying to ruin me?

SARA: He's joking.

MARC: I know, Mom.

SARA: You look great.

MARC: Thanks.

SARA: You put on a lot of muscle at that school.

MARC: Mom!

            Pause.

RON: We have to go out in a sec. I know how much you hate this stuff.

MARC: That was before

RON: - Before we go out, son, Marc: can you forgive us?

MARC: For—

RON: For sending you there.

SARA: It killed us to do it.

MARC: Listen. I'm not going to forgive you, not for a second. There's nothing to forgive. The only thing I want to do is to thank you. For loving me enough that you'd send me to Pine Grove—that's what I learned there, that you would be prepared to put yourself through agony so I could turn my life around.

RON: Which you have

MARC: - Which I have and that's the second thing I need to thank you for—for being the kind of parents that recognize that, and not sending me back. And in the matter of forgiveness—well, I should be begging yours—for my behaviour before.

RON: Why don't we all just forgive each other?

MARC: Sure.

RON:	The school really—you really feel changed? Inside too?
MARC:	A thousand per cent.
RON:	Because knowing that really makes my job easier. In what I have to say to out there.
MARC:	Good. Hey. They're calling for you. Time for your acceptance speech, Dad.

Scene 12
At the podium.

> *RON walks into the light. Streamers etc.*

RON: *(After a few thank yous.)* My friends, these last few months of minority government have been wild and woolly. I'm glad we have the opportunity to go back to the electorate now, with a clear plan, with a program in place—because we need to bring clarity and precision to the governance of this province and, to do that, we need a majority. It is important for you all to realize that, over the past few months, no matter how great the turmoil in the legislature, we never lost sight of our principles. And foremost amongst those: the core principle of any enlightened society: equality.

Scene 13
Outside the school.

> *Sounds of speechmaking and cheering off. MARC is leaning against the school wall. ZIMRAN appears. He is wearing his harq, but also has a political button and maybe some other kind of slightly inappropriate and uncool sign of independence, like sunglasses (at night) pushed up his forehead.*

MARC: Hey!

They do the handshake.

How come you're here?

ZIMRAN: Can't I be?

MARC: I didn't think you'd be into this kind of thing.

ZIMRAN: I came with my father.

MARC: Jesus—he's here?

ZIMRAN: It's a long story. He's supporting your old man.

MARC: No way.

ZIMRAN: Way.

MARC: I thought you guys didn't vote. I thought that was part of your religion.

ZIMRAN: We're into it now. And we're a hundred percent behind your Dad. Cool eh? It's important to support your friends.

MARC has pulled out a doob.

What're you doing!

MARC: What's it look like?

ZIMRAN: Are you out of your mind?

Scene 14
Inside the rally again.

RON: We recently began a process in this province that will bring equity to our schools. This is not universally popular—especially with the teacher's unions—those unhappy folk you saw picketing the meeting tonight—but it's a necessary one. We live in a diverse society. We have to acknowledge that, in an equal society, the freedom to educate your children according to your beliefs and culture is an inherent right. And it is now going to become a reality in this province, if we are re-elected.

Cheering, especially from ZIMRAN, who is off. RON may acknowledge ZIMRAN.

Scene 15
The studio.

Lights come up on BARBARA. Badly dressed.

BARBARA: Two weeks ago I was at the opening of the new school library in Plevna. I helped raise money for it and I can't tell you how gratifying it was to open that shiny new space full of books. I told the children a little story about a wonderful teacher I had at the public school there who told me that I should dream big, really big...

Scene 16
The rally.

SARA, then MARC have moved behind RON. A perfect tableau.

RON: ...But my friends. Let's not kid ourselves. This is going to be a heck of a tight election, especially here in Ashburnham. The Conservative vote in this riding is strong. It's going to boil down to what kind of candidate the NDP throws at us, how many votes they siphon off, but I have no doubt that, with your help, we will triumph, we'll take this fight for equality to the people and we will win.

Scene 17
The studio.

BARBARA: …She told me I could be a teacher or a doctor or a
                lawyer and I think if she'd known what an
                Executive Assistant was I'm sure she'd have said I
                could become that, too.

Scene 18
The rally.

                The perfect tableau has even been joined by
                ZIMRAN, who has moved in.

RON: *(As cheers rise.)* …So thank you all—have a great
                party tonight—and then tomorrow let's get out
                there and start working our tails off!

                They freeze.

Scene 19
The studio.

BARBARA: …But funny thing. The one thing my wonderful
                teacher never told me I could do—is run for public
                office. Become an elected politician. Be the MPP for
                Ashburnham. And that's ironic because, with your
                help, and that of my campaign team, that's exactly
                what I intend to be. Thank you.

                Pause.

                That's it.

BILL: *(Off.)* That's it?

BARBARA: Short and sweet.

                TV lights out.

                Thanks Bill. We can let ourselves out.

SAM appears. Comes up to BARBARA.

SAM: You done good, sister.

BARBARA: I managed not to swear.

SAM: No. The jacket's scary. We'll work on that. Steve's got some ideas. He thinks mauve might soften your edges.

BARBARA: Steve says I've got edges?

SAM: Honey, have you got edges. Now, where's the switch?

BARBARA: I'll get it. Hey. Funny thing.

SAM: What.

BARBARA is reaching for the switch.

BARBARA: It's on the left now.

She hits the house lights. For a second she is silhouetted in the hall light, and then stage goes to full black.

The End.

370- 13